LIFE CHANGING KINGDOM PRINCIPLES

AUTHORS FOR CHRIST

Copyright © 2023
Life-Changing Kingdom Principles
Authors for Christ

From a Collection of Various Gifted Christian Authors
Each author is separately named at the beginning of the testimony they have written. All testimonies are used with permission.

All rights reserved. No part of this book may be used or reproduced by any means, graphic, electronic, or mechanical, including photocopying, recording, taping or by any information storage retrieval system without the written permission of the publisher except in the case of brief quotations embodied in critical articles and reviews. Because of the dynamic nature of the Internet, any web addresses or links contained in this book may have changed since publication and may no longer be valid. The views expressed in this work are solely those of the author and do not necessarily reflect the views of the publisher, and the publisher hereby disclaims any responsibility for them.

ISBN-13: 9798857807408

All Scripture quotations, unless otherwise indicated, are taken from the: King James Version of the Holy Bible. All Scripture quotations are used by permission. Scripture marked (NKJV) are taken from the New King James Version®. Copyright © 1982 by Thomas Nelson, Inc. Used by permission. Scripture quotations marked (NIV) are taken from the Holy Bible, New International Version®, NIV®. Copyright © 1973, 1978, 1984, 2011 by Biblica, Inc.™ Used by permission of Zondervan. All rights reserved worldwide. www.zondervan.com. The "NIV" and "New International Version" are trademarks registered in the United States Patent and Trademark Office by Biblica, Inc.™

Editing / Interior Book Design & Layout / Book Cover Design
CBM Christian Book Editing
www.christian-book-editing.com

Printed in the United States of America

"WE OVERCOME BY THE BLOOD OF THE LAMB AND BY THE WORD OF OUR TESTIMONY." (REV. 12:11)

First and foremost, we dedicate this book to the Lord Jesus Christ, who is the Rock of Our Salvation. Thank you, Jesus, for the price that you paid. Thank you for your death, burial, and resurrection. Thank you for the Cross, Lord Jesus.

Secondly, this book is dedicated to you. May you find grace, encouragement, hope and abundant blessings as you read the wonderful teachings, testimonies, and stories within this wonderful book.

No matter what you may be going through, or what you are contending for, remember, in Christ, you are loved with an everlasting love, highly-favored, and precious in the sight of God.

We would also like to thank each of the authors who have participated in this book. Your testimonies are a blessing to read and share the love and redeeming passion that are available to all through Christ. As we have been blessed in reading your writings, we know that others will be also.

CONTENTS

KATIE MEADOWS 7
    WHAT UNRAVELING TAUGHT ME 7

CLINTON BEZAN 15
    DO YOU BELIEVE? 15

THELMA JANE 20
    THE EXISTENCE OF EVIL AND A LOVING GOD 20

HAZEL PINDER 28
    THE INHERITANCE 28

BRIDGET THOMAS 35
    EVERYONE HAS PROBLEMS 35

THELMA JANE 42
    GOD MAKES NO MISTAKES 42

MARY DETWEILER 49
    SUCCESS VERSUS PURPOSE 49

JEMAEL PARTLOW 55
    FORGIVENESS- THE HARD JOURNEY 55

ROBERT KURTZ 59
    HERE STANDS THE CHRISTIAN TEACHER 59

AMGAD SAMIR 69
    LIFE IN BABYLON: DANIEL AND THE SHIFT IN WORLDVIEW
    69

JEMAEL PARTLOW 71
    SPIRIT OF DECEPTION 71

DEBBIE COLE 77

MARY HAD A LITTLE LAMB 77
BRIDGET THOMAS **91**
    ONE PRAYER AT A TIME 91
BRIDGET THOMAS **98**
    A SECRET LIFE 98
GLORIA PIERRE DEAN **104**
    MENDING THE BROKEN 104
RICHARD CHRISTENSON **108**
DR. STEVEN GEORGE COY **115**
    A TROPHY BUCK TALE 115
LARRY CLAYTON..**123**
    THE FIRST GREAT SERMON IN THE NEW WORLD: ANTON DE MONTESINOS, 1511 123
JERRY McRAVEN **133**
    JESUS IS THE ANSWER.. 133
CHELSEA KONG **141**
    EXPERIENCE GOD'S PRESENCE 141

KATIE MEADOWS

WHAT UNRAVELING TAUGHT ME

Today is "one of those days." I've had a few of them lately. The pressures of life are a non-stop wave, crashing into my mental space and draining my emotions. As a believer in Jesus, I am acutely aware of my responses to environmental cues. I don't always get that right… but I am learning it's part of being human.

A Shaking

The past months have been heavy. A constant toll of personal issues, with unrelenting work pressures, and a wave of emotional and spiritual oppression, did some damage. I'm still standing. My armor may be dented, and my smile has dipped, but I am still standing. Praise God for the anchor of faith, securing me to that Rock of all ages. Without Him, I don't know how I would even crawl through another day (and yes, crawling is an option when you can't walk!).

I don't think I'm the only one. When I read online comments and listen to others' stories, a similar pattern emerges. Life is tough for many of us. Covid-19 shook the world, but during a global crisis of fear and isolation, individuals went through their own shaking. I consulted my personal writing to find:

She turned to me in a meeting and declared that the Lord would begin a shaking. I stared back. I knew that. Are you talking to me? I'm not the one to be shaken. The surrounding stuff of the world is to be shaken. Surely, you're referencing an event that the world has spiritually experienced many times over since Eve ate a lie? Why choose this moment to tell me?

I'm reaching. Why is everything on that top shelf so far away? Why can people experience the delirious delights of the third heaven so easily while I strain to see through a veil?

A shaking.

I just wanted a quiet life. The perfect Christian family, a kitchen full of produce and home-made comforts, and a picket fence were all I wanted. I'm now a Jubilee "plus" and the house with the picket fence is a distant memory. Nothing is perfect. (It is not true that WD40 and duct tape fix everything.) I see a future—dimly—but it's there. I see an end to the confusion and the juggling. But it's not enough anymore to just see it. I want to feel it—to live it! I want my destiny and I want it today. So, let the foundations of man fall. Let the hope of glory descend. Let the shaking intensify. Only that which God ordained will remain.

There are tremors of an earthquake in my soul.

Little did I know I was about to undergo a shaking! Adonai, the Master of this globe we call home, had a plan. While the world was reeling, my life had a parallel experience. And I believe God did this for many others—in fact, any who had ears to hear and a heart to receive. It wasn't comfortable, but for those of us who had cried out to Him for answers for months, years, or decades—He came through. He is still coming through.

The Unraveling

We became a new generation of onions—being unraveled, one skin at a time. The process of peeling an onion is tedious. Some onions are resistant. Some squirt you in the eye with their bitter juice. Others unravel quietly. The person doing the peeling and unraveling experiences the onion's mess—sometimes crying in the process. Is that how God feels when He gently and wisely unravels us?

I am grateful He goes at the pace I can cope with. Some realizations I've had recently have left me jarred—and then numb. I now know, over all the years I told Him to do what He needed to do (and quickly!), He knew best and has been preparing and protecting me. He knew the layers that needed to come off before I was ready for the next revelation and healing.

He reveals deep and secret things;

He knows what is in the darkness,

And light dwells with Him.

Daniel 2:22 NKJV

How many times have I prayed that God would shine His light into the darkness, and declare that the darkness must dissipate before it? Too many to count… but I believe He heard every prayer and has them recorded. Some of the "deep and secret things" are unpleasant, even shameful. We have our own sanctification to work out, but there is also a process of seeing in the dark—of discovering where we have been deceived by others, and where others have dealt treacherously with us.

This is a time of exposing. God is exposing the darkness and its sinister trail of abuse. He has always known what people do in secret. He gives us the opportunity to partner with Him to see what He sees—but there is a maturation process first. We can't walk wisely and maturely through these revelations without first being healed.

We need to understand that despite the horrendous things we discover in our lives, or the lives of our ancestors, love is the only way to view the truth. Without being cocooned in His love, we may lose our sense of identity, and we may become bitter and hateful towards those who hurt us. Bitterness will eat away at our soul.

So, how do we walk through life's storms, without succumbing to the waves that smash into us, or the slow and steady downpour of indoctrination? Here are several things the Lord showed me over time, as principles and strategies. These basics of the spiritual realm provide a compass and protection. I know and I trust they work, even if I cannot see anything. There are plenty of other weapons at our disposal, but I identify these as four core truths to remember and apply.

1. *Light separates from darkness.*

I can confidently pray the light of Jesus onto and into everything, knowing the darkness must flee. I know that "Let there be light" is a reality—that by the power of the Spirit in me, my words impact my environment and push the darkness back.

(Genesis 1, John 1, 1 John 1)

2. *I have heavenly armor.*

While some prefer to see Paul's armor reference as analogy only, I don't believe in a separation of physical and spiritual (despite my logical mind bucking at the idea!). This analogy is powerful when applied by faith. Christ's sacrifice truly purchased my salvation. I need that helmet of protection over my mind! Before I apply that helmet, I like to add the "mind of Christ". I know my mind is dull by comparison! The rest of the armor is powerful, and it is encouraging to remind ourselves of our spiritual standing, despite our physical reality.

3. *Living water refreshes me.*

I have only recently realized I've neglected my spirit! I believe a vast majority of Christians do, because we are so heavily focused on the soul realm. Western Christianity (the type I am used to) tends to make general references to our spirit, but focuses on our mind—that place of intellect, will and imagination. My mind is subject to attack! My spirit is secured for eternity.

Jesus offered living water to the woman at the well—a never-ending supply of spiritual refreshing. Living water is perfect to pray over the parched souls of humans, especially to prepare for the seed of the Gospel to take root. But it is beautiful and refreshing for our spirit. I am a triune person and I need to remember the part of me that most easily communes with my Father. Slowly, the light is dawning, that I need to live less from my soul and more from my spirit.

4. Tune in to kingdom frequencies.

God's creation resonates with frequencies that reflect His sound. His Holy Spirit and ministering angels speak and act in frequencies that resonate the sound of the Throne of Grace. God's kingdom sounds good! It is peaceful, loving, merciful, and safe. It brings us to repentance through humility, and it protects our fragile being.

The opposing spiritual kingdom uses frequencies, too. These frequencies are coming at us every day through multiple channels, and in overt and covert ways. Understanding spiritual kingdom dynamics has enabled me to pack more power in my prayer—and it's opened my eyes to what is really happening around me.

The danger of being nice

The late, great Derek Prince taught me some basics on witchcraft. Learning about witchcraft was heavy! I was raised in a conservative church, so I needed a crash course on how witchcraft manifests. It is not all broomsticks and Ouija boards. I spent months processing and digging in to teaching on the topic.

Far from sitting only in the realm of practising witches, the "craft" is all around us. Galatians 5:20 tells me clearly that witchcraft is a fruit of the flesh! From this place of revelation, words and actions take on a new dimension.

Every time someone tries to control us—what we think or how we act—they use witchcraft. Narcissism uses witchcraft to control another person, often resulting in tremendous abuse. Gaslighting is witchcraft.

It was painful to realize that people close to us often do this witchcraft—endeavoring, consciously, or subconsciously, to control how we think, feel, and behave. We can't blame everything on the devil.

Christians have been taught to be "nice". I've looked for this word in the Bible, without success! I can find words like compassionate, and kind—but never nice.

A substitute English teacher taught me that "nice" was applied only to things, never to people. You could have a "nice cup of tea", but you never had a "nice friend". I am thankful she highlighted this. It has come in handy! I am not called to be nice—I'm called to be wise and discerning.

Behold, I send you out as sheep in the midst of wolves. Therefore be wise as serpents and harmless as doves.

Matthew 10:16 NKJV

It's only from this place, I can see the truth. I lived so much of my life believing the best in people, because I was trained to "be nice". That didn't make me wise and innocent, it made me naïve and gullible. It made me susceptible to people taking advantage of me, including the enemy of my soul… (I'm still picking up some of those pieces.)

Wise and discerning people are sometimes not very nice! They don't allow the enemy an opportunity to wheedle his way in—they've often learned the hard way. They view people through the lens of love, with an extra prescription of discernment. Doesn't Paul say to the Church of Galatia:

*O, foolish Galatians! Who has **bewitched** you?*

Galatians 3:1 NIV (emphasis mine)

The wolves were mingling and pressing palms, wearing their best sheep costumes, and smiling knowingly into the eyes of their victims. This was no time to play nice. It was spiritual life or death. Paul didn't hesitate to call out their foolishness and address the witchcraft clouding their newfound revelation. This is a brilliant example of witchcraft in action—people tricking and manipulating people.

What if some wolves are friends—or family? Waking up to the realization that people close to you are not who you thought they were, is disorienting and heart-breaking. It distorts your sense of reality and leaves you reeling. Those closest to us can be the deepest source of hurt, betrayal, and confusion.

Even though I've had "one of those days" (or decades!) I know Who goes into my tomorrow, ahead of me. He prepares a table for me in the presence of my enemies. They don't get to dine with me—but they have a front-row seat to the banquet of the Spirit. Let my fruit be worthy, and my actions reflect what my mouth proclaims.

As the Lord readies to pour my drink, I pray for capacity to drink from the overflow. May I see in the dark, but not be afraid of it. May joy be my inheritance. I pray for the power of God's mercy and forgiveness to flow through me onto my enemies, that they would know Jesus is Lord.

And may I continue to praise Him, despite my circumstances.

And we know that all things work together for good to those who love God, to those who are the called according to His purpose.

Romans 8:28 NKJV

Author Biography

Katie Meadows is an Australian author, with a passion to see others develop into their full potential. Whether as a HR professional, or in the context of church community, friends and family, Katie enjoys investing in people. She has presented faith focused shows for her local Christian radio station and produces topical God-spots of encouragement. Teaching and writing became a passion following years of university studies and business operations. When she isn't working or writing, she loves doing life with her treasured family and friends. Katie and her husband live in Central Victoria with their children and grandchildren close by.

Books by this author:

Meat Pots, Manna, and a Merciful God: Exchanging the Wilderness for Promise

Contact the author at:

www.katiemeadows.life
journeypublishing@outlook.com

CLINTON BEZAN

DO YOU BELIEVE?

John 3:16 boldly proclaims, "For God so loved the world that He gave His one and only Son, that whoever believes in Him shall not perish but have eternal life." This is probably the most recognized, most quoted, most cherished and most misapplied verse in scripture. So the compelling question is, what does it mean to believe?

Is belief simply acknowledging the historicity of Jesus Christ and living with the same appreciation for him as other historic figures, such as Albert Einstein, Plato or Isaac Newton? Or does belief in Christ constitute completely embracing Him and everything He said as truth and compel one to live differently from those who don't believe?

This concept challenges the notion of saying one believes and the assumption that eternal life is granted based upon this confession whether there is evidence of repentance or not. So in this brief examination of what it means to truly believe in Jesus Christ I want to draw our attention to the Greek word used that is translated as "believe" in this particular passage of scripture.

The ancient Greek word used is *pisteuō* which stems from the word *pistis*, or "belief." The word *pistis* is derived from the word *peithō*, which means to persuade or to be persuaded. The word *pisteuō* implies deep trust and confidence. Trust is defined as: a firm belief in the reliability, truth, ability, or strength of someone or something.

So, when we read John 3:16 with this in mind, it means to trust in Jesus and have confidence in Him. It means that you are willing to risk your eternal destiny based upon His promise. It means that you will take to heart what He said and taught and live according to His words. It means surrendering to His lordship and being loyal to His sovereignty.

The disciples followed Jesus. They said they believed in him, yet when he was crucified, they scattered in fear and even denied Him. Judas betrayed Him. It wasn't until He resurrected that they entered into a state of trusting Him and being willing to die for Him. Jesus told Thomas, "Because you have seen Me, you have believed; blessed are those who have not seen and yet have believed." (John 20:29).

It is the comprehension of what it means to believe that reconciles faith and works. If faith without deeds is dead (James 2:17-26), then those who claim to believe in Christ, yet fail to exhibit evidence of being born again in the way they live are still dead in their sins (Ephesians 2:1-10). We are saved with the intent of doing good works and this signifies that our salvation is authentic.

Now, if we trust Jesus, we will trust His promise. John 14 begins, "Do not let your hearts be troubled. Trust in God; trust also in Me. In My Father's house are many rooms; if it were not so, I would have told you. I am going there to prepare a place for you. And if I go and prepare a place for you, I will come back and take you to be with Me that you may also be where I am." (John 14:1-4).

If we trust in Jesus we accept everything He said as truth. In John 8:31-32, Jesus said this: "If you hold to My teaching you are really My disciples. Then you will know the truth and the truth will set you free." And in John 15:4, He says "Remain in Me, and I will remain in you. No branch can bear fruit by itself; it must remain in the vine. Neither can you bear fruit unless you remain in Me."

Some translations use the word "abide" which comes from the Greek word *menō* and can mean dwell or rest. It means fully embracing Jesus and living for Him. John instructs us, "See that what you have heard from the beginning remains in you. If it does, you also will remain in the Son and in the Father. And this is what He promised us – eternal life." (1 John 2:24-25).

John continues in verse 28, "And now, dear children, continue in Him, so that when He appears we may be confident and unashamed before Him at His coming." One day we will all stand before Jesus and confess that He is Lord. As we anticipate that meeting, let us ensure that we are completely free of apprehension. In 2 John 1:9 we are told bluntly. "Anyone who runs ahead and does not continue in the teaching of Christ does not have God; whoever continues in the teaching has both the Father and the Son." There is no need to be unsure of where we stand if we remain faithful to Jesus.

"This is how we know we are in Him: Whoever claims to live in Him must walk as Jesus walked." (1 John 2:6). Abiding in Christ is the most fundamental attribute for those who profess to be Christian. The apostle Paul Wrote, "So then, just as you received Christ Jesus as Lord, continue to live in Him, rooted and built up in Him, strengthened in the faith as you were taught, and overflowing with thankfulness." (Colossians 2:6-7).

This means living our lives "dialed in" to Jesus. We facilitate this by reading His word, fellowshipping with other believers, Bible study, prayer and regularly worshipping with others and having communion with them. When we commit ourselves to focusing on Christ in these ways our thoughts will be dominated by what we have seen, heard and done as we contemplate what we have learned.

We then become living testimonies to the salvation that only comes through Christ Jesus. In 2 Corinthians 3:3, Paul likens this to a letter of recommendation, "You show that you are a letter from Christ, the result of our ministry, written not with ink but with the Spirit of the living God, not on tablets of stone but on tablets of human hearts." As children of Abraham (through faith) we inherit the promises of God's laws and through Christ we can have them written in our hearts and minds (Ezekiel 11:19; Ezekiel 36:26; Jeremiah 31:33; Hebrews 8:10). Not dead hearts but hearts and minds that have been made alive spiritually.

Paul instructed the church at Galatia to live by the Spirit (Galatians 5:16-17), and thereby not gratify fleshly or worldly desires. In essence this is also abiding in Christ, resulting in production of the fruit of the Spirit. "But the fruit of the Spirit is love, joy, peace, patience, kindness, goodness, faithfulness, gentleness and self control." (Galatians 5:22-23a).

When we live in this fashion, we will see Jesus in everything. And when we walk in this manner, we will be cognizant of the elderly woman needing a hand to get to her car and not walk by without helping. We will give generously to charities that help orphans and victims of violence and natural disasters. We will function from a premise of brotherly love and love for God and His Son.

Luke 8:16 records Christ's words, "No one lights a lamp and hides it in a jar or puts it under a bed. Instead, he puts it on a stand, so that those who come in can see the light." Unless Christians exemplify the love of Christ, they cannot bear fruit in a dark world. We are called to profess the truth and not to supress it. We are called to spread the good news of the gospel and unless we live in a way that conveys our belief in Jesus, we cannot show Him to others.

Similarly, in Matthew 5:14-16 Jesus taught, "You are the light of the world. A city on a hill cannot be hidden. Neither do people light a lamp and put it under a bowl. Instead, they put it on its stand, and it gives light to everyone in the house. In the same way, let your light shine before men, that they may see your good deeds and praise your Father in heaven."

When we abide in Christ, He abides in us. When we live in Him, He lives in us. When we become Christians the Holy Spirit enters into us and dwells within us (1 Corinthians 3:16, 6:19; 2 Corinthians 6:16;2 Timothy 1:14; and Romans 8:9, 11). In John 14:23, Jesus is recorded as saying, "If anyone loves Me, he will obey my teaching. My Father will love him and we will come to him and make our home with him."

These words are trustworthy and we can bank on the fact that when we truly believe in Jesus Christ we will never walk alone. When we are dialed into Him we can discern His instructions and respond in a meaningful way. James 4:8 confirms this, "Come near to God and He will come near to you."

When you live by the Spirit, your spirit will align with Him and you will experience intimacy with Him at the very core of your being. He will guide you to discipline your thoughts and subsequent actions and give you peace that transcends all understanding (Philippians 4:6-7). This transformation is repentance in action, and it cannot occur unless there is sincere and authentic belief.

Saying you believe and living your belief aren't necessarily synonymous. For one person Christianity can be simply a religion they identify with. It is a common perspective that lacks conviction (and the power to save). For another it is a "oneness" with Jesus that is so much a part of their life that it is at times difficult to determine where they end and He begins. This is the very same intertwined oneness that Jesus enjoyed with our heavenly Father and prayed for His followers to have (John 17:20-26).

Authentic belief is transforming belief. It is radical belief.

Author Biography:

Clinton Bezan is a compelling and authentic Christian apologist and published author proclaiming the truth of the Bible as God's word and the gospel of Jesus Christ. His unique appreciation and passion for Christ are evident in his answer to God's call to write.

Clinton maintains a blog website to interact with readers: https://www.partneredwithchrist.com/

THELMA JANE

THE EXISTENCE OF EVIL AND A LOVING GOD

"Those who know your name trust in you, for you, Lord, have never forsaken those who seek you." (Psalm 9:10 NIV)

Taking this and other scriptures into consideration that support this principle raises questions based on the following scenario.

Let's just say that someone broke into your home while God was visiting you. The intruder beats you to a pulp, leaving you for dead, ransacks your home then leaves. In the meantime, God, who was invisible to the intruder, sees everything that took place but did nothing to assist you in your time of need. Even humanly speaking people reach out in love to help save lives, one example being the horrific event that took place on 9/11/2001. Yet, we can't help but question how a God who is all powerful and loving can sit back and allow evil to exist in our lives and in the world.

First off, to say that God *allows* evil suggests that He can prevent evil, but in some cases He chooses not to as in the example of Job (1:6-22). Paradoxically God never chooses evil. Psalm 45:7 says, *"You love righteousness and hate wickedness."* In 1 John 1:5 it also says, *"God is light; in him there is no darkness at all."* Deuteronomy 32:4, *"He is the rock, his works are perfect, and all his ways are just.* ***A faithful God who does no wrong****, upright and just is he."* (Emphasis mine) Evil, however, is the *absence* of God's love, resulting from an *imbalance* to God's perfection, which began with the fall of Adam and Eve. Therefore, if God can prevent evil He does, but there are certain instances within His laws of love that will not allow Him to prevent evil.

One such example is freedom of the will, which enables one to make choices based on their own set of values and priorities. Humanly speaking we cannot see things from God's perspective, which obviously is why we make wrong choices, and why God wants us to trust Him. Why then did God *choose* to let Satan cause Job such pain and suffering? Job's love for God obviously had to be tested and refined by the fire which God allowed Satan to do by not interfering. There are other reasons beyond our understanding that bind (thwart) the power in God's love to prevent evil as in the above scenario.

The existence of evil can also be attributed to the necessity for God to reproduce after Himself, which He could not do without dying to the flesh revealed in His creation. The principle in God's Word that says: *"unless a kernel of wheat falls to the ground and dies, it remains only a single seed. But if it dies, it produces many seeds."* (John 12:24). Further reasoning shows that God could not reproduce Himself as One, but had to bring forth His Word in part. So first He reveals His law and then His love, which identifies with the Old and New Testaments of the Bible. This division in God's Word, however, creates an imbalance to God's perfection which resulted in the fall of man. 1 Corinthians 13:12-13 says, *"For now we see only a reflection in the mirror, then we shall see face to face. Now I know in part, then I shall know fully, even as I am fully known."* Knowing that evil would exist in the world, God could have refused to obey His laws of love in bringing forth the creation. But in so doing, His love revealed through the creation, would not have been made known nor could it survive.

In obedience to God's laws of love, as shown in the above paragraphs, God cannot always prevent evil. If He could, but didn't, He would not be a God of love. God does, however, use the effects of evil to overcome evil (the power of Satan in the law ruling the flesh) that is out to destroy us. In 1 Peter 5:8 it says: *"Be alert and of sober mind. Your enemy the devil prowls around like a roaring lion looking for someone to devour."* In Revelation 2:7 it also says: *"To the one who is victorious, I will give the right to eat from the tree of life, which is in the paradise of God."* Humanly speaking we *cannot* overcome the power of Satan in the law ruling the flesh. The flesh, opposed to God's love in the Spirit, is impatient (wants to be first), jealous (wants all the glory), envious (wants to be above all), proud (exalts itself), easily offended (cannot accept rejection). Its judgment and values are based upon the present (that which is evident), vulnerable to suffering (having no tolerance for imperfection), and demands respect (kind to those who obey its rule but will destroy those who rebel against its authority). This description supported in Galatians 5:17, refers to Lucifer, who after the fall of Adam and Eve became Satan, god of the material world. (Ephesians 6:12).

In 1 John 3:8 we are told. *"The one who does what is sinful is of the devil, because the devil has been sinning from the beginning. The reason the Son of God appeared was to destroy the devil's work."* Therefore if we are to get to heaven we must put our trust in Jesus Christ. *John 3:16 says, "For God so loved the world that he gave his one and only Son, that whoever believes in him shall not perish but have eternal life."* In Matthew 16:25 Jesus says: *"For whoever wants to save their life will lose it, but whoever loses their life for me will find it."* Further support to this principle is found in John 3:36 where it says: *"Whoever believes in the Son has eternal life, but whoever rejects the Son will not see life, for God's wrath remains on them."* The Bible makes it clear that there is *no other way* for us to be saved from the wrath of God for those who remain under the power of Satan in the law ruling the flesh. Since God has already won the battle between the flesh and the spirit through the cross of Christ, we can trust Him to pave the way for us to get to heaven. In John 14:6 Jesus said, *"I am the way and the truth and the life. No one comes to the Father except through me."* Is Jesus the *only* way to heaven, and if so, how can we be sure that we are headed in the right direction?

God Directs Our Paths

Principle in God's laws of love reveal that there are many roads that lead to heaven but only one door to God's kingdom, which is through Jesus Christ. The road we take, however, can be related to the different religions, which is an outward expression of one's faith in God. While God honors our faith in doing what we believe in our heart to be right, our religion may be taking us in a wrong direction. Yet we can be assured that if we are truly searching for God we will find Him, but may experience many pitfalls along the way. Examples include those who were misled by religious cult leaders such as Jim Jones, David Koresh and others. We may also parallel the different religions to what took place at the tower of Babel. In Genesis 11:7 *"The Lord said, "If as one people speaking the same language they have begun to do this, then nothing they plan to do will be impossible for them. Come, let us go down and confuse their language so they will not understand each other."* This principle applies to our communication with each other spiritually speaking, which has also led to the many different religions we have today with every religion believing they have the "keys" to God's kingdom. While religion serves a good purpose it is responsible for some of the most heinous crimes in the history of man, and continues to this day to cause division in families and in the world. Presently, however, from what is being prophesied a one world religious system, headed by the antichrist, is in the making. What this religion will be is not yet known, but we can be sure that it is man-made, which can be related to the tower of Babel, and not from God. The Bible warns that in the last days many will be deceived. Matthew 24: 23-24 says: *"At that time if anyone says to you, 'Look, here is the Messiah!' or, 'There he is!' do not believe it. For false messiahs and false prophets will appear and preform great signs and wonders to deceive, if possible, even the elect."* Other scriptures include Mark 13:6 *"Many will come in my name, claiming, I am he,' and he will deceive many."*

This deception brings to mind an experience I had when out shopping with my mother. I went into a store while she waited in the car. When I came out of the store I got into the car which was full of cigarette smoke. I thought it was strange since my mother didn't smoke but just sat there waiving my hand in front of my face trying to clear the air. In the meantime, I could hear a horn blowing but paid no attention until I looked over to the woman in the driver's seat who was just staring at me. Embarrassed and apologetic I got out of the car and could see my mother who was parked directly across from this woman, laughing at my mistake. She could have spared me of the embarrassment had she caught my attention before I got into the wrong car. The mistake, however, was easy to make since both cars were older models and identical. They were parked directly across from each other in front of the store, and ironically the other woman bore a resemblance to my mother which, in that case, was rather humorous.

That experience was only an example of how we can be fooled by look-a-likes. In my situation, I was able to distinguish the difference between my mother and the other woman. But how do we distinguish the difference between the Christ and the Antichrist if we are unable to recognize them? It appears that we are born with two sets of eyes, one being the physical and the other spiritual. In our search for truth, God opens our eyes spiritually so that we can recognize Him in the same way that we are able to recognize our physical parents. But before having our eyes opened to see God, we must be born of His Spirit as described in John 3: 1-7.

"Now there was a Pharisee, a man named Nicodemus who was a member of the Jewish ruling council. He came to Jesus at night and said, "Rabbi, we know that you are a teacher who has come from God. For no one could perform the signs you are doing if God were not with him. Jesus replied, "Very truly I tell you, no one can see the kingdom of God unless they are born again." "How can someone be born when they are old?" Nicodemus asked. "Surely they cannot enter a second time into their mother's womb to be

born!" Jesus answered, "Very truly I tell you, no one can enter the kingdom of God unless they are born of water and the Spirit. Flesh gives birth to flesh, but Spirit gives birth to spirit. You should not be surprised at my saying, 'You must be born again.'"

Once we are born of God's Spirit, *"The Spirit himself testifies with our spirit that we are God's children."* (Romans 8:16). Becoming a child of God is an honor but also comes with a responsibility that we should not take lightly. The following is a list of reminders to help you grow in the grace and knowledge of God. May the Lord bless you and strengthen you in your endeavor to serve Him.

1. You are the Temple of God's Holy Spirit. (1 Corinthians 3:16, 6:19-20).

2. Honor God in your word and deeds. (Colossians 3:17). If we don't place value on our own words we should not expect others to.

3. Be thankful in all things, and open to God's will in our prayers. Remembering also to thank Him *before* our prayers are answered as well as after. (Thessalonians 5:16-18).

4. Check your motives to make sure your desires are in right standing with God. (Psalm 26:2).

5. Fill your mind with God's Word by reading your Bible and thinking on His laws of love.   (Philippians 4:8; Psalm 1:1-2).

6. If you fail to obey God ask His forgiveness and to strengthen you spiritually. (Psalm 86:5; Daniel 9:9).

7. If you offend someone else ask their forgiveness (Matthew 6:14).

8. Be kind to those who may not be kind to you, leaving vengeance to God. Also pray for your enemy. (Romans 12: 19-20; Luke 6:27-28; Matthew 5:43-44).

9. Tithe. Give to God what you owe to God. (Proverbs 3: 9-10).

10. Do not forsake your fellowship. (Hebrews 10:25).

11. Keep focused on where you are going and not where you've been. As in running a race don't look back. (1 Corinthians 9: 24-25). *See yourself* as having *won* the race. (2 Timothy 4:7).

12. Remain strong in the faith knowing that there is *nothing* beyond our reach. (Luke 1:37).

13. Put your hopes in those things that are eternal and not temporal (Colossians 3:2; 2 Corinthians 4:18).

14. If you want to impress someone, be humble. (James 4:6).

15. Let the Holy Spirit be your guiding light and Jesus your suit of armor in your journey to heaven. (2 Samuel 22:29; John 16:13; Ephesians 6:10).

About the Author

Thelma Jane has been a born-again Christian for many, many years. She is a mother and grandmother as well as an award-winning hairstylist and devoted student of the Bible. She enjoys spending time with family and friends and has also enjoyed working with people on a one-to-one basis in the hair salon before her retirement in 2013. Thelma's inspiration for writing, however, was the result of her awareness of God's spiritual laws, which began at a very young age and deepened as she matured. After becoming a born-again Christian and reading the Bible she also realized that these were the laws that Jesus taught in His ministry and fulfilled through His death on the cross. And in them, there was all wisdom, knowledge, and truth. Through her insights into these laws, she believed she could shed light on some difficult questions in theology that led to writing her book, *The Soul's Destiny: Discoveries of an Ordinary Christian,* available on Amazon and other Internet book sites. Presently Thelma Jane is dedicating her time to writing articles and short stories as examples of how God's laws of love, like the physical laws of the Universe, apply to our lives. (© **Thelma Jane 2023**)

Excerpts taken from *The Soul's Destiny: Discoveries of an Ordinary Christian* **(Columbus, OH: Gatekeeper Press, 2022)All scriptures taken from the NIV Bible.**

HAZEL PINDER

THE INHERITANCE

Often, we read about our past being our heritage, and no more so than in the Church, the legacy of God's people down the centuries. Although, on many occasions, their history makes for uncomfortable reading, especially for the Israelites who often had a series of unwelcome events affecting their people. Left in Egypt, after Joseph, who was instrumental in helping Pharaoh save his nation from famine, died. Unfortunately, years later, the joy of the past was eroded as the weight of Egypt's power turned against them, forcing them to become slaves to the Egyptians; not quite what Joseph had envisaged, all those years before. Certainly, life has its twists and turns, which was certainly true for this nation, controlled in work that was grueling and harsh, having to live in ways contrary to their God.

Disillusioned, resentful, and abiding by a harsh law and work ethic, the Israelites undoubtedly absorbed the ungodly ways of their captors. Imagining that God had forgotten them as time went by, although this was far from the truth, as God had their interests at heart and wasn't oblivious to the fate of His people. Therefore, the cry from deep inside their hearts was heard by Him, one that he'd waited to hear for a long time, which was why He sent Moses to bring the salvation they needed.

Of course, we know the full story of how Moses led the Israelites out of Egypt with the Passover Plague, which killed the Egyptians' firstborn sons, and the rulers drowned as they chased after the Israelites through the sea.

It is an amazing story that depicts heartache and miracles, as God guides them through the wilderness, to establish a relationship with Him that took many years to accomplish. It was a time when awesome things happened, as Moses, directed by God, led the people through the desert until the stench of Egypt had gone from them.

It was during this time that God made a pledge, or a covenant with the people, a beautiful connection to God that included precious promises, that God wanted the people to uphold as they journeyed. It was through this experience that God showed them how to live united with Him, and to keep unsoiled from the wickedness of the world, as they honoured Him.

In many ways, it is a story of the foundation of our faith, when the law which we call the commandments, and the first five books – known as the Pentateuch or the Torah, were given to the people to live by. The fifth book, Deuteronomy, God revealed to Moses before he died, and it contains the blessings and curses. I haven't itemized the law or the blessings and curses, they are there in the Bible to read in Exodus, Leviticus, and Deuteronomy, all important parts of the root, or doctrine of the Church; certainly not to be pushed back in a drawer and forgotten!

We may ask ourselves, living in the twenty-first century is any of this relevant to the Church, or can we disregard it all?

Today we live in a world of illusion, where people search for truth through AI, forming relationships that seem real but are mere dreams, through their computer. Consequently, people live guided by their own desires, and holiness is not an expression or word that is understood; therefore, conduct is usually influenced by whatever emotion is felt at the time…and we see the reality of this when murder, the sanctity of life and so much more are blazoned across our newspapers.

However, our God is a reality, mighty and awesome, and sees all, therefore the guidance that God gives must underpin our belief. It was the code of conduct that was respected by the founding Fathers, or in many ways the backbone on which the Church is founded.

Today we reflect on this and learn from the Israelites and from Moses' lifestyle, which may alert us to question where we are heading today as a Church, after receiving such established truths to build on.

This might also pose a further question in our minds, as to wonder further if possibly some churches have lost their way, which is why what is written in Matthews' gospel, imparted by the Lord Jesus Christ, is vital to consider...

Matthew 5 verses 17-18 (NIV), "Do not think that I have come to abolish the Law or the Prophets; I have not come to abolish them but to fulfill them. I tell you the truth, until heaven and earth disappear, not the smallest letter, not the least stroke of a pen, will by any means disappear from the Law until everything is accomplished."

Learning from the past is a wise way to live, and although we live within the new covenant of salvation in the New Testament, the law is God's standard and we value it and endeavor to live guided by it.

If the Lord stated He came to fulfill the law, we must, as a church, recognize its importance. If we do not, that is called rebellion, for all who flout God's way and are intent on doing their own thing. God gave the laws, all those years ago, to turn the Israelites from doing things in their own strength, and to give them guidelines to live by, because He understands human nature.

On writing this piece I had a picture of the Church as it is today given to me, which I want you to imagine. It is a picture of the way the Church is being tempted and enticed by the world.

The picture depicts the Church in an extremely deep and vast hole, that is miles wide with steep high sides.

***Around the** top of this vast hole, circling and waving, are bright flags and pennants fluttering the enticing allures of today. There is a noisy rabble shouting down to the people at the bottom of the hole to come up, out of the Church. The people at the top, are part of organizations endeavoring to seduce Christians with their beliefs. They are shouting down to those deep below who are in the Church, to come up and join them. There are vast numbers of these folk surrounding the Church below, stretching for miles and miles at the top of this vast hole. Bright flags that flutter with all kinds of persuasions, as people keep screaming down, denoting their presence and organization. Inciting the Church below, to accept them and to embrace their principles and policies. It is a noisy* *situation, as the people circling are never silent or still, tossing pamphlets down, while shouting out their creeds to woo all of those who will listen. Many ladders are trailing over the top of the abyss, and lots of* **people climb up and down**

This is a simple message and a vision that has been laid on me to share, a prediction of where the Church is heading, and, sadly, how some churches function today. Realistically, the Church has not set itself apart and is now keen to embrace modern teaching that is totally opposite and contrary to God's way making the Church unholy. Church leaders, concerned with declining numbers, discard the past and use methods that relate to the twenty-first century. The sad fact is that in doing so the Bible and God are being replaced, or watered down, and this plays into the hands of the enemy of truth, who hates God and tries to inflict all kinds of anomalies on God's people, which is why we must continue to explore God's words such as in the book of John, to find truth.

John 1 verse 14 (NIV), "The Word became flesh and made his dwelling among us. We have seen his glory, the glory of the one and only Son, who came from the Father, full of grace and truth."

This speaks of the Lord Jesus Christ who was fully God, and fully man, who walked this Earth and remonstrated with the money lenders in the Temple, against their using His Father's house as a marketplace. The Redeemer, who holds the entire foundation of Christianity in His hands gave His life in humility, as a precious sacrifice for cleansing healing, and salvation, delivering a New Covenant that supplants all that has gone before.

Hebrews 7 verses 26-28 (NIV), "Such a high priest truly meets our need—one who is holy, blameless, pure, set apart from sinners, exalted above the heavens. Unlike the other high priests, he does not need to offer sacrifices day after day, first for his own sins, and then for the sins of the people. He sacrificed for

their sins once for all when he offered himself. For the law appoints as high priests' men in all their weakness; but the oath, which came after the law, appointed the Son, who has been made perfect forever."

Amazing news, no longer do we look for cleansing as they did in the Old Testament, in the time of Moses when the priest applied the blood, and a sacrifice was made to cleanse and heal the people. The book of Hebrews explains clearly how today's Church has been blessed with the New Covenant through the blood of Christ.

Hebrews 8 verses 7-12 (NIV), "For if there had been nothing wrong with that first covenant, no place would have been sought for another. But God found fault with the people and said "The days are coming, declares the Lord, when I will make a new covenant with the people of Israel and with the people of Judah. It will not be like the covenant I made with their ancestors when I took them by the hand to lead them out of Egypt, because they did not remain faithful to my covenant, and I turned away from them, declares the Lord.

This is the covenant I will establish with the people of Israel after that time, declares the Lord. I will put my laws in their minds and write them on their hearts. I will be their God, and they will be my people. No longer will they teach their neighbour or say to one another, 'Know the Lord,' because they will all know me, from the least of them to the greatest. For I will forgive their wickedness and will remember their sins no more."

This was the gift that the Lord Jesus Christ gave, an amazing sacrifice by the Son of God who came from Heaven for all people. Once we realize this, we do not ever assume anything…we realize just how powerful and awesome our God is. Who must never be questioned or made to be weak or humanised, He is Adonai, our Lord and Master.

Unfortunately, today, the awe of God seems to have become neglected, while the Holy Spirit's leading tends to be in mere words and seldom a demonstration of His power. Sadly, once churches act in this way, they often choose to diminish the Word of God, allowing creeds and doctrines to become dominated by modern ethics as

Scripture is watered down. The reality being quite clear, that modern belief considers boundaries or standards are unnecessary, making it difficult to see the difference between the people of the world, and those following **Christ**.

It's strange because a chef has laws of hygiene that he never deviates from, because it would be dangerous to health. Simply put, surely the Church must realize, that once we weaken and change Scripture, we are damaging the church and causing offence to God, which is an awesome revelation.

2 Timothy 3 verses 16-17 (NIV), "All Scripture is God-breathed and is useful for teaching, rebuking, correcting, and training in righteousness so that the servant of God may be thoroughly equipped for every good work."

Our acceptance of the Bible is so important because it is the foundation for all Christian doctrine and belief. It is God's written word to mankind and everything a Christian believes comes from within the pages of Scripture. The Bible is our written assurance of God and the principal and belief of our faith and doctrine, therefore our faith or belief as Christians must agree with what is written in the Bible and balance the Old Testament with the New Testament.

Romans 7 verses 6-7 (NIV), "But now, by dying to what once bound us, we have been released from the law so that we serve in the new way of the Spirit, and not in the old way of the written code. What shall we say, then? Is the law sinful? Certainly not! Nevertheless, I would not have known what sin was had it not been for the law. For I would not have known what coveting really was if the law had not said, "You shall not covet."

I return to Moses as I finish. He was a man who loved God and learned obedience, although like us he made mistakes. A man whom God trusted, loved, and revealed His ways to, on many occasions. Through Moses' obedience so much was unlocked for the future that has benefitted the Church. And now through our Savior the Lord

Jesus Christ, we can come to an even greater intimacy with God. A pathway that was forged through the precious blood of Christ, making it plain that we can't live like the Israelites in Egypt, and must rid ourselves of all that is unholy that the world has taught us.

Therefore, we do not forge our own pathway, but embrace the truth of Christ in humility, as we walk in obedience with our God, anointed by the Holy Spirit. Always recognizing the sheer awe and power of our God, as we read in Acts, He will have His way, because He is powerful and astounding, a totally overwhelming God, which is why we must heed the Bible.

Consequently, for those that do not do so, they will fall by the way and find out that Hell is real, which is frightening.

Acts 28 verses 26 -27, (NIV), "Go to this people and say, 'You will be ever hearing but never understanding; you will be ever seeing but never perceiving.' For this people's heart has become calloused; they hardly hear with their ears, and they have closed their eyes. Otherwise they might see with their eyes, hear with their ears, understand with their hearts and turn, and I would heal them."

Isaiah 5 verse 15 (NIV), "So people will be brought low, and everyone humbled, the eyes of the arrogant humbled. But the Lord the Almighty will be exalted by his justice, and the holy God will be proved holy by his righteous acts."

There is little time left, we have a small window of opportunity- what are you doing with your life today, are you going to stand for Christ or walk the way of the world? - The choice is yours.

Hazel E Pinder

Author of ***Cyronus, The Treasures of the Kingdom* and *The Promise of Heaven,* and an "Author for Christ"**

BRIDGET THOMAS

EVERYONE HAS PROBLEMS

"Everyone has problems," my husband said into the phone. He was talking to his sister and sharing some of the troubles that we had been dealing with. And my sister-in-law also shared some of the things that her family was facing.

We all do have different problems on different levels. Some seasons of our lives feel harder to bear than others. Some days feel hopeless. Some days our faith waivers. Some days we are weak with the weight of our worries.

However, it doesn't have to be this way. Yes, there will always be problems on this earth. Yet we don't have to lose our hope or our faith.

But this begs the question - how do we make it through? You have heard of the saying "one day at a time." I am adopting a different spin on that - "One Prayer at a Time." That is the key to surviving through tough times.

One thing I have discovered is that in troubled times we have a choice. Problems can either tear us down, or we can choose to draw closer to God. We can choose to cling to Him in prayer. We can choose to trust Him.

I know it's not always easy, especially because it seems like when it rains it pours. Many times, it's not just one problem we are dealing with, but several. When we are bombarded with various troubles, we might feel as though we can't keep our heads above the water that is pouring down.

That's when we choose to stop fighting the waves and surrender into the arms of the Lord. He is our lifeline. According to Oxford, a lifeline is "a thing on which someone or something depends or which provides a means of escape from a difficult situation." That is exactly what God can be for us during difficult times. But we have to make that choice to draw near to Him. And I have found that prayer is vital to stay afloat.

Prayer brings us comfort during difficulties. Throughout any given day we will face tasks that we don't want to deal with, bumps that suddenly arise in the road, unexpected situations that come our way, and more. So how can we survive when we feel like we're walking through a landmine? One prayer at a time.

In 1 Thessalonians 5:17 it says to "pray continually." Some Bible translations say to "pray without ceasing." We might wonder - how do we pray without ceasing? That seems like an impossible task. But I have found that talking with God all throughout the day, and praying for strength and guidance in each situation – this brings peace in the midst of the storm. This echoes what Paul told us in Philippians 4:6-7: "Do not be anxious about anything, but in every situation, by prayer and petition, with thanksgiving, present your requests to God. And the peace of God, which transcends all understanding, will guard your hearts and your minds in Christ Jesus."

And something that amazes me is how God is always there, ready to listen to our every word. When I was a child, my maternal grandparents lived over a thousand miles away. When I was very young, my grandfather passed away. At the time, my mother traveled to be with my grandmother and spent a few months with her. Returning home worried my mother because she felt as though she was leaving my grandmother all alone, far away from everyone.

This prompted my mother and grandmother to start a new routine. This was when everyone had landlines and mobile phones were unheard of. Every single night before heading to bed one of them would ring the other one's phone and hang up. Then the recipient of the initial ring would ring back and hang up. Some nights my grandmother got to it first, so she would ring and hang up. My mother would then dial my grandmother, let her phone ring a couple of times, and hang up. Other nights my mother might have gotten to it first, so the order was reversed. Of course, if one of them felt like talking that night, then they would answer the phone, let the phone keep ringing, or maybe even call back. But the majority of nights, they would ring and hang up.

This went on for around fifteen years, until it was time for my grandmother to live with my mother. The ring each night was a message letting my mother know that my grandmother was safe, she was okay, and all was well. And it also gave my grandmother a way to connect with someone each evening, since she lived alone at the time. The ring of the phone provided a sense of comfort to both parties. The ring of the phone was all they needed to go to bed each night in peace.

We too can have comfort and peace every day and every night of our lives. We don't have to ring someone like my mother and grandmother did. We can turn to Jesus in prayer. No matter how alone we might feel at times, we can feel connected to our Lord and Savior every single day. No matter what is weighing on our minds, we can rest assured knowing that He is there. We can connect with Him at any given time.

We don't have to wait to see if God will ring back or answer the phone. He will always be there. And He always hears us when we call on Him. Sometimes it might feel as though God is not listening, but that is never true.

I love reading in the Psalms. They bring me comfort and joy. And I am especially intrigued when I see a theme in the words. When reading through the Psalms in 2020, during a time when the whole world was anxious from the pandemic, I was amazed at how many verses I found that assured me that God hears us when we call. I would like to share some of those verses with you.

- "Know that the LORD has set apart his faithful servant for himself; the LORD hears when I call to him." - Psalm 4:3

- "In the morning, LORD, you hear my voice; in the morning I lay my requests before you and wait expectantly." - Psalm 5:3

- "You, LORD, hear the desire of the afflicted; you encourage them, and you listen to their cry." - Psalm 10:17

- "I call on you, my God, for you will answer me; turn your ear to me and hear my prayer." - Psalm 17:6

- "In my distress I called to the LORD; I cried to my God for help. From his temple he heard my voice; my cry came before him, into his ears." - Psalm 18:6

- "I sought the LORD, and he answered me; he delivered me from all my fears." - Psalm 34:4

- "I waited patiently for the LORD; he turned to me and heard my cry." - Psalm 40:1

- "You who answer prayer, to you all people will come." - Psalm 65:2

- "You answer us with awesome and righteous deeds, God our Savior, the hope of all the ends of the earth and of the farthest seas." - Psalm 65:5

- "But God has surely listened and has heard my prayer." - Psalm 66:19

- "The LORD hears the needy and does not despise his captive people." - Psalm 69:33

- "When I am in distress, I call to you, because you answer me." - Psalm 86:7

- "I love the LORD, for he heard my voice; he heard my cry for mercy." - Psalm 116:1
- "I call on the LORD in my distress, and he answers me." - Psalm 120:1
- "When I called, you answered me; you greatly emboldened me." - Psalm 138:3
- "The LORD is near to all who call on him, to all who call on him in truth." - Psalm 145:18
- "He fulfills the desires of those who fear him; he hears their cry and saves them." - Psalm 145:19

These are just a few promises found in the Bible, which tell us that God hears us, He is there when we call, and He answers us. If we cry out to Him, pray to Him, praise Him or even just whisper to Him - He always hears the voices of His children. And more than that, He answers. What a wonderful gift we have in prayer.

I mentioned that I love reading the Psalms. I also love reading the Gospels. Not only do they provide us with an inside look at our Savior, but they also show us how we are to live when we follow Him. One theme I have seen in the life of Jesus was how much time He spent in prayer. Luke 5:16 is one example where it says, "But Jesus often withdrew to lonely places and prayed." When I read verses like this, I have to wonder - if this time alone with the Father was vital for Jesus, how much more important should it be for us?

I admit that when I was a young Christian, I didn't put enough weight in prayer life. Thankfully, as I have grown closer to the Lord, He has shown me how valuable prayer is. I see now that prayer is so much more than something we check off of our to do lists. Prayer is not something we *have* to do; prayer is something we *get* to do. Prayer is an honor and a privilege. We are able to meet with our loving Father at any time and from anywhere.

And something that astonishes me is that I can see how in prayer I am being shaped and formed to be more like Jesus. We are molded into the person God purposed us to be when we meet with Him in prayer. Prayer helps us to shed the gunk of this world as we are transformed from the inside out. Whether we are crying out in despair, whispering words of gratitude, calling out in praise, or begging for divine help - He is there. He is eager to hear from us. He listens to every word. And He is happy to help us and wrap us in His loving arms.

Spending time with God in prayer also helps us to learn more about Him. We begin to understand how incredibly merciful and faithful He is. We are filled with awe at His goodness. His love fills a void deep within our hearts.

When we sit in God's presence and have a conversation with Him, we are forming a strong bond and a meaningful relationship. God is incredibly fond of us and longs to hear from us. Through prayer we not only receive strength, help and guidance, but we also receive love and tender care. May we remember the priceless gift we have in prayer.

I may not know what you are facing today. I may not know what you have been dealing with in this season of your life. But one thing I do know is that God is only a prayer away. He is there for you. He is ready and waiting for you to call upon Him. He loves you beyond measure. And He wants you to reach out to Him. And He will hear every word. He will get you through whatever you are facing – one prayer at a time.

Dear Heavenly Father, I admit that stress has been bringing me down. But I turn to You in prayer, today and every day. You alone can help me. You give me strength, hope, and courage. I put my trust in You. I hold onto the words in Psalm 118: 6 - "The Lord is with me" (NIV), "The Lord is for me" (NLT), "The Lord is on my side" (NKJV). What comfort those words bring. Thank You for always being there for me. Thank you for always hearing my prayers. I hand all my stress over to You. I know this doesn't mean I will never have any problems. But it does mean I can lean on You through it all. Thank You, God. I am so thankful for You. I praise Your Holy Name and I love You. In Jesus' beautiful name I pray, Amen.

About the Author

Bridget A. Thomas is the author of Every Day is a Gift, You Are Redeemed, and Giving God Your Whole Heart. She lives in Florida with her husband and two fur babies. Her obsessions are Jesus, books, and coffee. Bridget and her husband enjoy watching baseball games and traveling to the Smoky Mountains. To learn more about Bridget, visit her at bridgetathomas.com.

Every Day is a Gift!
Bridget

THELMA JANE

GOD MAKES NO MISTAKES

"'For My thoughts are not your thoughts, neither are your ways My ways;' declares the Lord. 'As the heavens are higher than the earth, so are My ways higher than your ways.'" Isaiah 55:8-9, NIV

Jay and I thought the adoption process would be fairly easy, but we were in for a surprise to learn that it wasn't as easy as we had thought. Though many babies need homes, adoptive parents are carefully screened to find the right family for each child. However, when Jay and I decided to adopt we went through a reputable agency in our own community. A friend who held a high position in the community and worked indirectly with this organization offered his support. We filled out all the paperwork initially required by the agency which included the age and gender of the child we were seeking to adopt. Jay and I prayed for a newborn baby girl but we were open to other possibilities if the Lord had another child in mind for us. After a two to three month waiting period, we were informed that a mistake was made in the process of reviewing our application, for which they had apologized. A child, however, had not yet been assigned to us. When our friend became aware of the mistake the agency made, he was upset and offered to assist us in getting the problem resolved. But we assured him that it must not have been in God's plan for us to go through with the adoption.

Sometime after that experience Jay and I decided to seek international adoption with the hope of adopting a baby girl from Korea. The process included meeting every month with the social worker and other couples also seeking to adopt a child. Those meetings were informative and challenging. We were given different scenarios of what problems might arise with children coming from a different culture, especially an older child. There were also strict rules applied to the age of the adoptive parents. In our case, we could not adopt a child under the age of three since Jay did not meet the requirements for a newborn. However, after having completed the classes and all the paperwork involved we were put on a waiting list.

Within the next couple of months Jay and I received a call from our social worker letting us know they had a child for us. "What is her name and how old is she, I asked?" We were expecting to hear that the child was a three year old, but was totally surprised when told that we were assigned a newborn, which was an answer to prayer. It appears that the mother went into a midwife home, had the baby and left. We accepted the adoption, but there would be a six month wait before our baby could be released from the country of her birth. Possibly this was to allow time for the mother to return for her child. Our baby, however, arrived three months earlier than scheduled. This was a very memorable time as our Pastor, family and friends joined us in celebrating the arrival of our daughter who came to us from Soul Korea.

Taking the above into consideration, not only supports the principle that God directs our paths as stated in Proverbs 16:9, but that our lives are mapped out for us before we are born. Psalm 139:16 says, *"Your eyes saw my unformed body; all the days ordained for me were written in your book before one of them came to be."* Knowing that Kristen was destined to be our child, Jay and I believed that her biological mother was *like* an angel of the Lord who brought Kristen to us and then disappeared. Our convictions were also confirmed that Kristen's biological mother would not return since she came to us before the six month waiting period was up. It may also be mentioned here that while Jay and I were extremely grateful for the friend who extended himself to assist us in the process of adoption, ultimately God was in control. Psalms 19:21 says, *"Many are the plans in a person's heart, but it is the*

Lord's purpose that prevails." This principle is also supported in Isaiah 14:24. "The Lord Almighty has sworn, *"Surely, as I have planned, so it will be, and as I have purposed, so it will happen."* In addition to God's plan in adopting Kristen, we received an extra blessing that would not have been made known to us without God's intervention. While in Soul Korea, we had friends who visited the home where Kristen stayed before coming to Jay and me. From the pictures we received Kristen appeared to be perfectly healthy and well cared for in those first few months after her birth.

Having heard this story since she was a baby, Kristen also has the assurance that Jay and I are truly her parents for which, she said, she has been grateful. Believing that it was in God's plan for her to be our child, Kristen has not searched for her biological parents, but admits she would be interested in knowing something about her genetic background mainly for health reasons. Kristen has grown up to be the best daughter that any parent could hope for, and now has her own daughter who is also a beautiful and loving child. Our family will always be grateful to the adoption agency for placing Kristen with us and to the Lord for His guidance and direction, every step of the way, in the adoption process. God's plan for our lives, however, is further supported in the following story.

A Blessing in Disguise

Eleanor was an older woman who was adopted when she was a baby. Growing up she had all the comforts of a nice home and loving parents. She was a kind and caring person who was married and had children of her own. Eleanor, however, did not know that she was adopted until later in life. She attributes this to a few reasons. One- being born at a time when some things were kept more secret. Some parents feared disclosing that information to their child for fear of the affect it may have on them. The concern, of course, would be that they would hear it from someone else. That did not seem to be a problem in Eleanor's case since no one else seemed to know that Eleanor was adopted or if they did, nothing was said. She reminisced about having a big family with lots of cousins whom she grew up with, but did not have a close relationship with them.

One day, however, Eleanor called to ask if we could go to lunch. When we met that afternoon she seemed sad and depressed. I asked Eleanor if she was ok and she said she wasn't. So I asked if she wanted to share the burden she seemed to be carrying, with me and she nodded, yes. That's when I first learned that Eleanor was adopted but didn't understand why she was so sad until she explained the reason. She went on to say that she recently learned that her biological parents had four children, two boys and two girls and she was the only child that they gave up for adoption. Her adoptive parents were distant relatives, and the children who she thought were her cousins were her brothers and sister. Though Eleanor loved her adoptive parents and was very grateful to them she felt hurt and rejected to know that her biological parents chose to give her up. I could certainly sympathize with Eleanor, and encouraged her to put her trust in the Lord, but she was led to believe that God had also turned His back on her.

However, in the course of conversation I asked Eleanor how her brothers and sister were doing. Her response was, from what she had heard, "not very well." It appeared that she came from a very dysfunctional family, which led me to believe that God was merciful to spare Eleanor of the pain and suffering that her siblings may have experienced while growing up. Yet the question that haunted Eleanor was *why* her biological parents rejected *her*, and if God did intervene, *why* did God choose to *spare her* and not her siblings? These are very legitimate questions that we might be able to answer if we could see the fuller picture of our existence through the eyes of God. Yet, we can be assured that God will do what is just and right for those of us who put our trust in Him. Jeremiah 29:11 says, *"For I know the plans I have for you," declares the Lord, plans to prosper you and not to harm you, plans to give you a hope and a future."* But we must also do our part in using our blessing wisely as stated in Matthew 25:14-30. Further assurance is given in the following scriptures.

God is fair. *Romans 2:11 says "For God does not show favoritism."* Yet in Romans 9:14-16 we are also told that God will have mercy on whom He chooses. *"It does not, therefore, depend on human desire or effort, but on God's mercy."*

We attract everything that happens to us (even *before* we are born), yet God is in control. Proverbs 16:33 says, *"The lot is cast into the lap, but its every decision is from the Lord."* Other scriptures support the principle that no one can make a decision for or against us without God's approval. Lamentations 3:37 says, *"Who can speak and have it happen if the Lord has not decreed it?*

We are always in the right place at the right time. *"The Lord makes firm the steps of the one who delights in him; though he may stumble, he will not fall, for the Lord upholds him with his hand."*(Psalm 37:23-24) *"In their hearts humans plan their course, but the Lord establishes their steps.* (Proverbs 16:9). *"A person's steps are directed by the Lord. How then can anyone understand their own way?"* Proverbs (20:24)

God will not abandon us. *"Though my father and mother forsake me, the Lord will receive me."* (Psalm 27:10). *"Have I not commanded you? Be strong and courageous. Do not be afraid; do not be discouraged, for the Lord your God will be with you wherever you go."* (Joshua 1:9)

God makes no mistakes. Psalm 18:30 says, *"As for God, his way is perfect: The Lord's word is flawless; he shields all who take refuge in him."*

Taking the above into consideration we are greatly responsible for creating our own destiny according to God's will for our lives. God, however, remains in control like a parent who puts their child on a leash. That is to say no one can ever go so far from God that they exist as a *separate* entity. Yet we can remain estranged if we choose to rebel against His authority in our lives. God wants to be our architect in designing our eternal home by trusting the blueprints He has given to us in the Bible. Or we can continue to design it ourselves which will not be the home we would want to live in eternally as described in Matthew 7:24-26.

Conclusion

In Romans 9:15, we are told that God shows mercy to some and not others as in Eleanor's case. Yet He is also a just God. (Psalm 89:14). When viewing our existence from a worldly perspective things seem unfair. Humanly speaking we judge outwardly which is why Proverbs 3:5 says to *"Trust in the Lord with all your heart and lean not on your own understanding."* We can also be assured of the scripture that says *"And we know that in all things God works for the good of those who love him, who have been called according to his purpose." Romans 8:28.*

Copyright © 2023 Thelma Jane

Note: The names and some details in Eleanor's story have been changed to protect the privacy of those involved. All Scripture has been quoted from the NIV Bible.

About the author

Thelma Jane has been a born-again Christian for many, many years. She is a mother and grandmother as well as an award-winning hairstylist and devoted student of the Bible. She enjoys spending time with family and friends and has also enjoyed working with people on a one-to-one basis in the hair salon before her retirement. Thelma Jane's inspiration for writing, however, was the result of her awareness of God's spiritual laws, which began at a very young age and deepened as she matured. After becoming a born-again Christian and reading the Bible she also realized that these laws were biblical principles that revealed wisdom, knowledge, and truth.

Through her insights to these laws, she believed she could shed light on some difficult questions in theology that led to writing her book, *The Soul's Destiny: Discoveries of an Ordinary Christian,* available on Amazon and other Internet book sites. Presently Thelma Jane is dedicating her time to writing articles and short stories as examples of how God's laws of love, like the physical laws of the Universe, apply to our lives.

MARY DETWEILER

SUCCESS VERSUS PURPOSE

As one moves into adulthood, it is important to establish a firm foundation upon which to live one's adult life. Part of establishing that foundation is making decisions about one's adult lifestyle and values. One of the decisions to be made is whether we will live a successful life or a purposeful life.

Regarding success, one can choose to adopt parents' and/or culture's definition of success because it fits one's own abilities, talents, interests, etc.; or one can choose to adopt parents' definition of success to please parents. On the other hand, one can choose a definition of success different from that of his or her parents to rebel against parents, or one can develop a definition of success that is different from one's parents' definition because it fits for him or her. The operative word here is *choose*.

Though many people in the world define and measure success according to the level of one's wealth, power, fame, and/ or status, these are not the criteria everyone uses to define and measure success. Some choose alternate definitions of success. Some of these alternate definitions are:

• "Success is getting up one more time than you fall down." (Lina Ramos)

• "Success isn't about how much money you make. It's about the difference you make in people's lives." (Barack Obama)

• "Success is liking yourself, liking what you do, and liking how you do it." (Maya Angelou)

- "Success is the ability to go from one failure to another with no loss of enthusiasm." (Winston Churchill)

- "Success isn't how much money you have. Success is not what your position is. Success is how well you do what you do when nobody else is looking." (John Paul DeJoria)

The first step in the process of choosing your definition of success is embracing the belief that you *have* a choice; that you are in charge of your life and can set the direction or course of your life. If you do not embrace this belief, you give that choice away, allowing others to chart the course of your life.

The next step is becoming aware of the lens through which you view the world. Each of us, whether we are aware of it or not, views reality through a lens comprised of values and beliefs about ourselves and our world. The values and beliefs that comprise our lens have their roots in what we were taught and what we experienced in the family and culture we grew up in. Though we may not be aware of our lens, it is most definitely there, and it works powerfully. It filters what we see and determines what we think about what we see. This includes how we define success.

Once you are aware of your lens, you can choose to either keep the values and beliefs that comprise your lens, or you can choose to delete some or all of them and insert values and beliefs of your own choosing. Again, the operative word here is *choose*.

If you're unsure how to go about developing your own definition of success, Stephen Covey has a rather unique suggestion as to where you might start: "If you carefully consider what you want to be said of you in the funeral experience, you will find your definition of success." (Stephen R. Covey, *The 7 Habits of Highly Effective People* (New York, New York: Simon & Schuster, 1994), page 140)

Another definition of success is: "Success is knowing your purpose in life, growing to reach your maximum potential, and sowing seeds that benefit others." (John C. Maxwell)

Regarding purpose, purpose is not one of the elements that comprise our lens. Our purpose does not come from what we were taught and what we experienced in the family and culture we grew up in, our purpose comes from God. He assigns it to us and designs us to be able to effectively fulfill it. Therefore, the starting point in choosing our definition of success is radically different than the starting point in understanding our purpose.

The starting point in choosing our definition of success is ourselves. When attempting to understand our purpose, the starting point is God. God created each one of us for a specific purpose, and he gave us the abilities, talents, interests, and spiritual gifts to fulfill that purpose. We choose our definition of success, either consciously or unconsciously, and we choose how to measure success; we do not choose our purpose. God chooses our purpose and then calls us to it. Though we don't choose our purpose, we do choose whether to respond to God's call and fulfill the purpose he chose for us.

When we choose to fulfill our God-assigned purpose we become fully who God created us to be. We then experience an unshakeable internal peace and joy that is beyond human understanding or attainment. It is the peace and joy that can come only from God. It lives below our feelings and does not change when our circumstances change.

Jesus doesn't want us to live a mediocre life, i.e., a life characterized by mere comfort, or worse, boredom or pain or fear or depression or frustration. He doesn't want us to live in survival mode, just making it, just getting by day by day. He wants us to live abundant lives. "'I came that they may have life, and have it abundantly'" (John 10:10 RSV). It is important to remember though, that the abundance Jesus referred to is not financial or material abundance. It is an abundance of life. He wants us to live a life in which we are happy, fulfilled, energized, and passionate.

He also wants us to live a life of peace. This peace is not an external peace in relationships, communities, countries, or the world. It is the unshakeable internal peace that lives below our feelings and does not change when our circumstances change. During the last meal he shared with the apostles before his crucifixion, he told them, "'I am leaving you with a gift—peace of mind and heart. And the peace I give is a gift the world cannot give. So don't be troubled or afraid'" (John 14:27). As the meal was ending, he said, "'I have told you all this so that you may have peace in me. Here on earth you will have many trials and sorrows. But take heart, because I have overcome the world'" (John 16:33).

Important Note: Jesus did not tell the apostles that their external lives would be peaceful. He told them their lives would have many trials and sorrows and that their peace would be in him. So, when we trust Jesus and keep our eyes (our spiritual eyes) on him, we will have internal peace regardless of what is going on in our external world. How do we obtain this peace? By fulfilling God's purpose for our lives.

There is another side to this whole concept of fulfilling God's purpose for our lives. That is, we are not the only ones who lose when we fail to discover and fulfill our purpose. Due to the system of human interdependence that God designed, everything we do or fail to do affects others. By not discovering and fulfilling God's purpose for us, we not only miss experiencing the peace and joy that only God can give, but others miss out as well. As Rick Warren states, "God designed each of us so there would be no duplication in the world. No one has the exact same mix of factors that make you unique. That means no one else on earth will ever be able to play the role God planned for you. If you don't make your unique contribution to the Body of Christ, it won't be made." (Rick Warren, *The Purpose Driven Life* (Grand Rapids, Michigan: Zondervan, 2002), page 241).

I wish I could say that once I put Jesus in the driver's seat of my life, I left him there. Regrettably, that is not the case. There have been times when I put myself back in the driver's seat, doing life my way.

Growing up, I learned that other people's opinions were very important. I learned that their opinions were the source of my self-worth. I, of course, didn't realize at the time that I was learning these things; still, I grew into an approval seeker and people pleaser *par excellence*!

As I walked with Jesus, my understanding of where my worth came from slowly changed. He taught me that my self-esteem and self-worth do not come from the approval of people. It comes from my relationship with him. I am a child of God, and therefore I have worth. As this truth took root in me, I began to see that the approval of human beings is unimportant and irrelevant. The only thing that is important is God's approval, which I already have by virtue of being his child.

Though I was living my life for an audience of One, at times I slipped back into my old pattern of seeking the approval of human beings to bolster my self-esteem. This would eventually blow up in my face, and I would remind myself that I no longer need to do that. As I am already assured of God's approval, I do not need the approval of human beings.

When I allowed God to be in the driver's seat of my life, I experienced the peace and joy that can only he can give. When I put myself back in the driver's seat of my life, I was looking for that peace and joy to come from human achievements and human relationships. What I received were the peace and joy that the world gives. Having experienced both scenarios, I can tell you that the peace and joy that the world gives are hollow compared to the peace and joy that God gives. Nothing can compare to that deep certainty you feel when you know you are right where you are supposed to be, doing exactly what you were created to do.

This article is comprised of excerpts from my book *When Success Isn't Enough*. If interested, you can find this book, as well as my other books on my blog/website isntenough.wordpress.com or my amazon author page https://www.amazon.com/-/e/B08KMYRZ72?ref_=pe_1724030_132998070

JEMAEL PARTLOW

FORGIVENESS- THE HARD JOURNEY

Forgiveness is a hard thing to do, and then bitterness sneaks its way in, rotting a person from the inside out. So how do we forgive? People talk about it, preachers preach about it, but it seems the people who seem to demand it, are people who haven't gone through too much. These people seem to talk about it like a *Nike* logo and you just do it, but instead, it's more like a complex math problem. Not all thieves steal materialistic items, for some thieves steal peace, wholeness, innocence, self-esteem, worth, value, healing, and/or closure. They come into a space that is not their's and they damage it, leaving a mess behind for you to clean up and do damage control. They destroy something that is not their's and leave behind massive holes and dark places, like an underground cave. They leave behind fear, insecurity, pain, and sometimes life-long emotional scars.

Some people believe you simply forgive, and that act is a demand and command you give yourself and it is done. I think that sometimes that is true if someone stole your doughnut out of the break room or the tires off of your car (see what I did there?), but if someone did something more distressing, then it requires more. Or, a small thing like that can activate things on a deeper level, from past hurts, making forgiveness harder than you might think. Something like that can bring up feelings from patterns in your life of being taken advantage of, not being respected, or being picked on. I believe sometimes, forgiveness comes from a journey of healing or a decision at the end of that journey, while others believe you forgive first to allow that journey to begin. Both are valid, but again, I think it depends on the level of damage that was done and the person. I seem to hear a lot of men be the ones that seem to think you forgive first and that is that. Men and women are different in their thinking and what they need. So maybe for a man, that is all there is, but that seems superficial and forgiving on a surface level (again maybe men are different as my husband disagrees with me and seems to think it is the old healing vs. forgiveness dispute). But for me personally, coming from my experiences, to truly forgive, one must start to take those demons that were left behind and face them one by one.

As an SA survivor, there is a level of pain that that sinks deeper into every aspect of you. Your innocence, your helplessness, your trust, a deep seeded fear, insecurity, and everything about you is stunted in growth and you cannot get that back. Your sense of self-esteem, worth, and value- frozen in time. Then our SAVIOUR comes and rescues us from the abuse the enemy has created, snatches our identity back from the enemy, and restores our value, worth, and self-esteem. Forgiveness from this seems to not be the main goal at first as you heal, but instead, facing the blackness that was left behind from that person. There are times the perpetrator themselves dissolves into nothing when it comes to traumatic experiences, and only the darkness they left behind remains the enemy.

In order to forgive, I brought forth all the crimes that were committed against me to GOD and asked HIM where HE was, and HE showed me. I brought before HIM the times I was stomped on repeatedly until that person's legs were tired, as I would curl up into a ball trying to protect my tiny eight year old body. The HOLY SPIRIT showed me how HE was there. There were no broken bones or serious damage, but merely minor bruises and sprained wrists and ankles each time. I saw a hedge of protection being formed around me as I never really felt the pain. HE showed me how HE planted the right people in my life, while removing others. HE showed me how much it upset HIM too and did not just stand there watching like a bystander, how HE already had things in place. HE comforted me and supported me in my healing process. The more HE held me with each crime, the more I healed, and the more I could forgive and let go. Not because they deserved it, but because I did. They did not deserve a space or place in my life, a place where they got to live in me forever. They took a piece of me but they do not get to reside in me and effect me or my life. The Bible is full of places where it says forgive and I think that is to help us, so it does not rot our bones from the inside out. It is to free ourselves and to heal so we can be healthy and not allow that to conquer us. I think GOD wants us to live free lives without the burden and heaviness of someone else's evilness. Their vileness is their's and their's alone to carry. There is a feeling of empowerment in placing that back onto them and allowing a just and righteous GOD to take care of them.

I once left a job because the bullying turned a corner and became abusive. I read a scripture one morning on how these types of women revel in hurting others (Isaiah 27:11). I felt the HOLY SPIRIT speaking to me and telling me HE understood my pain and would take care of them, but I am to forgive and move on. I do not need to carry that resentment and bitterness that will in turn, cause me to have pride and rebelliousness. Those things will eventually be used by the enemy to turn those things around and eventually blame GOD. In this one moment, GOD asked me to forgive by once again letting me know HE understands my pain that came from this, to let go of the bitterness, and to let HIM take care of them. Once I felt that, it was easier to let go and forgive. Now when I drive by that company, I am no longer a prisoner of anger, but I pray for them with sincerity that they know GOD one day. HE also showed me how my Christianity was what was being attacked, though they did not realize it, and GOD told me to wipe off the dust from my feet and move on.

GOD has taken me down different roads to get to the destination of forgiveness. Each being a different offense, none being the exact same, but each had to be intentional on my part. Abuse can lead to psychological damage and also brain damage, rendering forgiveness harder to do than in other circumstances. So in order to take this path, the HOLY SPIRIT lead me down different roads full of healing in order to forgive. As each place or piece was healed, I was able to let go of everything in it's entirety and that led to forgiveness. As each stone of pain was turned over, I was able to examine it, begin the healing, and then the forgiveness followed. Whether after the journey, or a decision I had to make for my own well being when the journey was over.

There were times that I misinterpreted forgiveness for numbness and/or acceptance, for I thought I had forgiven, but I had not. This is when we need to ask GOD to examine our hearts and help us to forgive others if we have not. They do not get to hang onto us and keep us psychologically, because we deserve to heal, forgive, and let go of that pain, becoming survivors instead of victims. Take GOD's hand today and allow that healing to begin as HE walks that journey with you, allow GOD in on your healing process and watch as hate, bitterness, and pain, slowly fall away, entering into the fullness and freeness of forgiveness.

JEMAEL PARTLOW

I have been married for 25 years and we have three great adult children! I enjoy being outside and that includes kayaking, hiking, swimming, paintball, traveling, and hunting. I like to read and enjoy digging into the Word! I have learned so much these last few years and seeing the Bible like never before. I have done speaking events and hold small annual conferences. I am a certified Christian mentor as well. I have started a support group for women whose husbands or children have mental health issues, and I am excited to see what GOD has in store for me down the road!

Jemael Partlow is author of: *GOD's Love, GOD in My Fire*

ROBERT KURTZ

HERE STANDS THE CHRISTIAN TEACHER

Where should independent school boards and administrative bodies look for qualifications that deem a person fit to teach in a Christian school? Certainly not to the secular arm of education, but to qualities expounded upon in the Word of God. Our intention is to give a clear idea of what God's Word suggests regarding the necessities of truly effective teaching. Since it is the expectation of parents that their children be guided by those who have testimony of life's pathway well trod, it would be inconceivable that a non-Christian or nominal Christian teacher be given the responsibility to mentor these children in biblical precepts and beliefs necessary to produce disciples of Christ. Following are Old Testament qualities for biblical teachers which are also applicable for today's educators.

Have a heart felt desire to teach, or to prepare the heart to teach. (Exodus 35:34; Ezra 7:10)

James Riley Estep Jr. pinpoints a central issue when he states: "We are not called to be Christians and educators but Christian educators." 1 This statement reveals the heart of this issue: Christian teachers need the calling of God in order to fulfill God's desire in their lives to be effective Christian educators. In any profession, if the heart is not in the fulfillment of that profession, the person will be effectively unhappy and unproductive. It is certainly not the desire of any Christian educational institution to employ anyone without a heart dedicated to following Christ and a deep desire to teach others of the reality of his/her heart relationship with a loving God. Ezra depicts this heart desire in Ezra 7:10 "For Ezra had prepared his heart to seek the law of the Lord, and to do it, and to teach in Israel statutes and judgments." (KJV) The heart is the core of biblical relationship. Jesus wants us to "love the Lord your God with all your heart, soul and mind." (Matthew 22:37 LB) Without that heart desire to love God, how would it be possible to teach students biblical values and truth? "For where your treasure is, there will your heart be also." (Matthew 6:21 KJV) If Christ is the teacher's treasure and pointing students to a living relationship with the Savior is his/her heart's desire, then lives will be impacted positively by the life and teaching of the teacher. The teacher's purpose will then be fulfilled living out that heart felt desire to teach.

Filled with the Spirit of God. (Exodus 35:31)

Christian teachers represent Jesus Christ in their every day walk. Therefore, in order to truly represent Christ to their students, God's Spirit must reside himself within their inner being. Scripture tells us that "all who are led by the Spirit of God are sons of God." (Romans 8:14 LB) Paul gives us a separation of man's knowledge and God's knowledge as he writes to the Corinthian church:

> For what man knows the things of a man except the spirit of the man which is in him? Even so no one knows the things of God except the Spirit of God. Now we have received, not the spirit of the world, but the Spirit who is from God, that we might know the things that have been freely given to us by God. These things we also speak, not in words which man's wisdom teaches but which the Holy Spirit teaches, comparing spiritual things with spiritual. But the natural man does not receive the things of the Spirit of God, for they are foolishness to him; nor can he know *them,* because they are spiritually discerned. (I Corinthians 2:11-14 NKJV)

So, it is evident that in order to teach the things of God in an educational setting, the Spirit of God Himself must indwell the teachers. Otherwise, only man' intellect will rule the classroom.

Filled with wisdom. (Exodus 35:31)

Wisdom has a Godly character to it. We are instructed that "if any of you lack wisdom, let him ask of God, that giveth to all men liberally." (James 1:5 KJV) The World Book Encyclopedia Dictionary denotes wisdom with these qualities: "knowledge and good judgment based on experience, scholarly knowledge." Synonyms related to wisdom are given as "erudition and prudence." Further elucidation shows erudition as "acquired knowledge, especially in literature, languages, history; scholarship; learning" and prudence as "wise thought before acting; good judgment". How necessary for the Christian teacher to have these qualities.

Is understanding. (Exodus 35: 31)

God also can give us understanding as reflected in I John 5:20 (KJV): "And we know that the Son of God is come, and has given us an understanding, that we may know him that is true, and we are in him that is true, even in his Son Jesus Christ. This is the true God, and eternal life." With this assurance of this understanding, it provides teachers with a solid foundation of a personal experience with the Lord and the opportunity to share this with their students.

How necessary for Christian teachers to have an understanding spirit when dealing with the needs and aspirations of students today. Paul encourages the Christians at Colosse, just as teachers today need what is emphasized in Colossians 1:9-10: "For this cause we also, since the day we heard it, do not cease to pray for you, and to desire that you might be filled with the knowledge of his will in all wisdom and spiritual understanding: That you might walk worthy of the Lord unto all pleasing, being fruitful in every good work, and increasing in the knowledge of God."

Is knowledgeable. (Exodus 35:31; Psalms 25:4-5)

David pours out his heart to God in desiring His knowledge: "Shew me your ways, O Lord, teach me your paths. Lead me in your truth, and teach me: for you are the God of my salvation; on you do I wait all the day." (Psalms 25:4-5) If Christian teachers exemplify this same desire to gain a knowledge of spiritual things, then their knowledge of secular subjects as well will resonate with their students. This teacher's life is built on a firm foundation of God's Word, therefore, any educational materials and life experiences he/she will share with the student will more likely be regarded as relevant and applicable to their life as well. It is indicative of today's students that their teachers' display of knowledge ability in their subject area is viewed with extreme importance.

Is skillful in workmanship. (Exodus 35:31)

It is well known that a great teaching environment does not guarantee learning without great teaching. Conversely, a great environment cannot substitute for lousy teaching. Skill in methodology, skill in presentation, skill in working the classroom, skill in individual assistance and direction, skill in passing on the excitement of pursuing knowledge, skill in presenting Christ daily through one's lifestyle, skill in caring, all help fulfill the workmanship of the Christian teacher. Paul reminds the Ephesian church that "we are his workmanship, created in Christ Jesus unto good works, which God has before ordained that we should walk in them." (Ephesians 2:10) It behooves the Christian teacher, created in Christ Jesus, to perform acts of good works toward the students they serve.

It is marvellous thought that a creative God uses His creation, the teacher, to employ creative methods to bring an exciting education to learners created in His image, so they may come to a personal knowledge of the Creator's Son, Jesus. To do this, committed teachers must cooperate with the Holy Spirit, establish interpersonal relations and mutual respect with their students, who in turn are encouraged to develop their individual uniqueness and creativity given them by a loving God. This creative atmosphere is penned by Shelly Cunningham as: "stimulating, emotionally safe and nurturing" as learners get "to make sense of God's Word [in] God's world". 2

Ability to judge the difference between what is holy (sacred) and what is unholy (ordinary). (Leviticus 10:10 KJV)

In our secular and pluralistic society where liberalism pervades, Christian witness and divine guidance is of particular importance to young people who so easily can be deluded into believing Satan's lies regarding the blur between what is holy and what is acceptable, but in reality, is not holy at all. Christian teachers can be pivotal in developing this judgment.

Teach the difference between what is pure (clean or good and right) and what is impure (unclean or wrong.) (I Samuel 12:23 KJV)

Samuel, in speaking to the children of Israel, shows his leadership qualities in proclaiming that he would not sin against the Lord by ceasing his prayers for them, but he would "continue to teach you [them] those things which are good and right." (I Samuel 12:23) Christian teachers have a God given duty and responsibility to pray for their students, and in the process of asking for guidance from God, would be able to teach them what is good and right. In an evil world, students deserve guidance into what is pure/good and how to distinguish it from what is unclean and wrong.

To teach the statutes of the Lord as given to Moses. (Leviticus 10:11 KJV)

When one thinks of Moses, automatically the 10 Commandments come to mind. Although we live in the age of grace, in the New Covenant, the laws given Moses were central to the godly living of the Israelite nation. Since there is a direct link between Old and New Testaments, God's desire would still have us live according to His precepts and instructions as presented in Holy Writ. His essential command would still spring forth from His instructions: "that you may teach the children of Israel all the statutes which the Lord has spoken unto them by the hand of Moses." (Leviticus 10:11)The New Testament emphasizes the eternal reward of such instruction in Matthew 5:19: "but those who teach God's laws and obey them shall be great in the Kingdom of Heaven." Could Christian teachers do less today?

Being teachable. (Psalms 119:66)

He who cannot be taught, cannot teach. David illustrates that he is most willing to be taught good judgment and knowledge. He further admits his belief and trust comes from God and His written word. His prayer continues, "Let my heart be sound in your statutes; that I be not ashamed." (Psalms 119:66, 80 KJV) Effective teachers in Christian schools today need a soundness in their own Christian experience in Christ and to not be afraid or ashamed of sharing the goodness of God with students entrusted to their care and mentorship.

What teachers should do.

Aspire to Inspire

Into whatever profession one enters there are always aspirations attached. In the teaching profession those aspirations accompany the desire to teach. Whether the aspirations target being the best teacher in one's school, becoming a highly motivated principal or advancing to the level of university where a professorship is the dream, the ultimate aspiration should be to inspire one's students to learn. After all, the end result of any teacher's lesson, encouragement, challenge or rebuke, should be to inflame the student's inner being with the inspiration to learn. To enjoy and pursue knowledge should remain one of the teacher's main aspirations, to inspire the student to learn.

Inquire to Acquire

Inquiry of the Lord and his Word by a Christian teacher, to improve his/her spiritual temperature and to procure educational sources to enrich their area of expertise, will definitely have a positive effect on students to acquire like-minded attributes demonstrated by their teachers. Enriching students' lives to desire to acquire greater spiritual maturity and educational acumen should reflect each Christian teacher's desire to serve their students' greater good.

Model to be modeled

As Christians, each teacher's heart throb should be like Paul as he addresses the Philippians: "Finally, brethren, whatsoever things are true, whatsoever things are honest, whatsoever things are just, whatsoever things are pure, whatsoever things are lovely, whatsoever things are of good report; if there be any virtue, and if there be any praise, think on these things. Those things, which you have both learned, and received, and heard, and seen in me, do: and the God of peace shall be with you." (Philippians 4:8-9 KJV)

Courage to Encourage

The psalmist David has great advice for all Christians, however, the true Christian teacher could take solace in his words: "Wait on the Lord: be of good courage, and he shall strengthen your heart: wait, I say on the Lord." (Psalm 27:14 KJV) "Be of good courage, and he shall strengthen your heart, all you that hope in the Lord." (Psalm 31:34 KJV) With this supernatural strengthening of heart, Christian teachers will be courageous in encouraging their students to further strides in their person pursuit of God and of the knowledge which will see them succeed in their personal careers and daily walk with the Master.

Implore to Explore

Teachers are from time to time challenged by certain students who are reticent to learn. In these cases, it behooves the teacher to implore those students to explore the many possibilities that educational resources have for them. In undertaking projects, they need to be encouraged to explore on their own, utilize group situations to collaborate findings and gain knowledge from their peers. So much information is available through the internet that a teacher must find ways of enticing students into areas of study that are interesting to them. Exploring new horizons of technology may just set aflame the student's desire to continue to pursue subjects that will enhance their lives and point them into life-changing directions.

Enthusiasm to Excite

Enthusiasm is infectious. Teachers who exhibit this infectious quality cannot but have a positive influence on their students. A Christian teacher, particularly, who is in love with the Lord and dedicated to the task of exciting students in their educational journey, will infect and motivate students to pursue their acquisition of knowledge and develop a lifestyle that will be pleasing to the Saviour.

Persistence to Pursue

Most teachers, to have arrived at their God given career of teaching, have had to be persistent in their pursuit of their educational goals as well as persisting in their Christian walk. Because they have experienced this necessity of persistence, they are better able to encourage their students in their pursuit of life, life-skills and perseverance to fulfill God's calling in their lives.

Passion to promote Compassion

Passion is great when directed in a positive manner. Rebellious and misdirected passion for godless desires leads to devastation and sinful consequences. Christian teachers with a passion to teach godly principles and a desire to engender a compassion within students for their fellow students or friends who do not know the joy of having Christ in their lives as Saviour, guide, and counsellor, will cherish observing the outplaying of this compassion.

Option to Optimize

There is no teacher alive that does not rejoice when students reach their optimal potential. As Christian educators, we have the option of accepting mediocrity (in our teaching and in our student's work), or of encouraging, challenging and maximizing students' opportunities to learn. Let us choose the option to optimize each student's ability to succeed, to rise to new heights, to see and contribute to their world with a Christlike spirit and a desire to add their personal accomplishments to the benefit of their community.

To illustrate important scriptures that focus on a teacher's influence, Paul clearly states: "The only letter I need is you yourselves! By looking at the good change in your hearts, everyone can see that we have done a good work among you." (II Corinthians 3:2 LB) He further says: "We boldly say what we believe [trusting God to care for us], just as the Psalm writer did when he said, 'I believe and therefore I speak'." (II Corinthians 4:13)

A Teacher Perception

A question is often asked: How will the Christian Education teacher differ in this century from what they have been perceived to be in the 20th century? Greg Bitgood, a superintendent of independent schools, exposed many interesting nuggets in my interview with him. The 21st century teachers bring an entirely different skill set than their predecessors. They bring with them a far different posture toward culture, which is not necessarily a good thing. Often because of societal pressure, they are over sensitive and tolerant to particular ideologies. A more open minded stance on moral issues is evidenced, at times too open-minded. In younger teachers, Bitgood senses a lack of biblical literacy and a much more relativistic approach to the interpretation of Scripture. As mentioned above, they have acquired a far better technological skill set than the older teachers. He feels that present day teachers are better educators, but not necessarily better Christians. 21st century teachers are better resourced, better encouraged, and better enabled to become more qualified. Due to the communication revolution, they engender a broader ability to communicate. Students today enjoy the first REAL digitals coming into the classroom.

Written by Robert (Bob) Kurtz, EdD, PhD.

The article was taken from his Kindle book "Selected Persons And Events That Have Influenced Christian Education Down Through The Centuries."

The author was a teacher both in Saskatchewan and Yukon Canadian educational systems for sixteen years. Responding to God's call to missions, he became a high school principal in Kenya, a Bible College Principal in South Africa, a lecturer in Colleges and Seminaries in Zambia, Zimbabwe, India and Nepal over a span of 25 years.

Footnote:

1 Estep, James R. Jr., Anthony, Michael J., Allison, Gregg R., A Theology For Christian Education, B & H Publishing Group: Nashville, 2008, p. 294.

2 Cunningham, Shelly, Introducing Christian Education Foundations For the Twenty-first Century, Baker Academic: Grand Rapids, 2001, p. 142.

AMGAD SAMIR

LIFE IN BABYLON: DANIEL AND THE SHIFT IN WORLDVIEW

In a sermon on last Sunday in a local church, the pastor spoke from the book of Daniel about 'life in Babylon '. He imagined how it was like for the Jews who were exiled to Babylon. On reflection, our small congregation living in a small town in regional Australia could see similar challenges confronted the Jews of the Bible thousands of years ago. At the time, the tiny nation of Judah was surrounded and overwhelmed by the struggle between the superpowers of the day, Egypt and Babylon. Eventually the small and weak kingdom was conquered by the mighty force of Babylon and the vast majority of the people were taken into exile.

A cultural shock is not even close in my imagination to describe this drastic change. I think it was something closer to a nuclear explosion that shook the core of the Jewish identity. Being 'God's chosen people' who lived in the land of Israel for hundreds of years, the Jews thought they were immune. They thought that their temple and their culture would protect them. Yet now, they are war captives exiled in a foreign land. They have no hope of return whatsoever except for a prophecy given by Jeremiah who was the same prophet who prophesied the doom and gloom on their kingdom. Probably many of them started questioning their faith, their tradition and their worldview. Where is God from his chosen people defeat? Where is God from all this suffering? Why is God allowing a blood-thirsty evil king like Nabuk Nazar get his own way and succeed?

Probably others questioned their culture on looking at the much more advanced civilisation of Babylon. I would imagine that seeing the mighty temples and the vast green gardens by the The Tigris and

The Euphrates rivers was grandiose and mind-blowing. Probably they looked down on themselves and felt how backward they were. They probably told themselves how stupid being a Jew was. Overall, there had been a dramatic and total shift in the norms and facts to these unfortunate people. Somehow, we resemble the Jews of those times in many ways. We may not be war prisoners but we are surrounded by a rapidly changing world that witness a major shift in morals, technology, religion, science and more.

This overwhelming change makes we wonder and question the worldview we held till very near past that we can all remember a few decades ago. We are like the Jews in Babylon. We are surrounded by a new world different from the past that we were so accustomed to and almost took its persistence for granted. That change definitely is leading many of us to ponder some questions, difficult questions that we would rather run from. Where is God? Why do evil powers prevail? What is right and wrong? Did we ever know what right and wrong were? Did we misunderstand the world? Where to go forward. Here looking at the lessons from history, scriptures and evolution come handy to help us navigate this uncharted water of time.

JEMAEL PARTLOW

SPIRIT OF DECEPTION

I was in a ladies' bible study group for years, and I enjoyed every bit of it. I enjoyed the atmosphere, the fellowship, the digging into GOD's word with my baby spoon that slowly, and eventually, turned in to a knife and fork. The physical food was a plus too! We were a group that I revered as what GOD intended women to be and look. We were loving, supportive, and we were friends bonded in JESUS. There were times we did not even have bible study if someone was going through something, including myself. We would lay hands, pray, and just love on that person through their trial. I had never really dug into GOD's word before, so I did not have a good understanding of it, so this was get. This started a love for GOD's word in my belly that only grew. I had always enjoyed worshipping and praying and even reading the bible, but this was deeper than just reading it.

After years of our ladies' bible study, life happened, and it dwindled and changed, but I still went. I began to notice that I did not enjoy the bible studies' as much from a biblical stand point. I always enjoyed the ladies, but I began to disagree with every bible study (there was always a book and video) and I did not know what was wrong with me. I became angry at myself for being so critical, judgmental, and negative. What was wrong with me?! I could not seem to help it, and I could not understand why I was being this way at all! I could not stand myself and how I was sabotaging the thing I had considered precious to me! While the other women were loving it and enjoying it, I would be stewing on how wrong the person in the video and book was. It would be in the back of my mind and nag me the whole time. I prayed and asked GOD to help me, but to no avail. Why would I allow one or two wrong things, or maybe just things that I disagreed with, keeping me from enjoying it? Maybe I was the one who was actually wrong, and I tried to look at it from that angle, but I could not seem to fix this heart problem.

Around this time, my husband and I were looking for a new church, and we had been at this particular church for about a year. There was an incident in which I was treated badly, and it upset even my kids, but I ignored it, for I was not there for the people in the church. The pastor was always energetic and I always learned something, even if I did not always agree. I believe it is good to hear different opinions, pray about it, and ask GOD for discernment; for I have been wrong before and that is how I grow! Then one day, the pastor was preaching something that hit my spirit so wrong. That began a series, where something was really wrong with his sermons. They had taken a wrong turn. Other people were even checking in on me to make sure I did not believe what he was preaching, for they had heard about it. His sermons had peaked negative feedback in my whole town, which is not small. I found myself becoming angry and negative in every service, just like I had in the women's bible studies'.

I was sweeping the kitchen floor one day, and I dropped to my knees as the HOLY SPIRIT fell on me like a ton of bricks. I spontaneously began doing intercessory prayer for the pastor. I cried with such force and emotion, that was unusual for a person I did not know, and had not even really met (it was a big church). I felt GOD's love for him and his love for the LORD, as HE pressed it into me. I cried out in desperation for a man I did not know, and I was being used in a spiritual way, interceding for him. I felt the demon of deceit that had fooled this pastor, and how the pastor did not realize it. I felt GOD wanting to remove this demon from his life and free him so he could see. There was no feeling of judgment or criticism; but only love for a man who loved his SAVIOUR, and the love JESUS had for him, and wanting to free him from this deception. (If you have read my previous article, I too have been deceived by the enemy, as we all have! It is an honor to be used by the HOLY SPIRIT to help each other out, as others' have helped me!)

Somewhere around this time, I had watched *The Chosen,* which led me down my own journey of learning the Jewish culture and how it pertained to the bible and JESUS. It took me about six months to do this study and I learned so much! I had regained my passion and fire for the bible again! Around the same time, the event with the intercessory prayer for the pastor took place, I went back to the women's bible study. They were also doing a study on how the Jewish culture relates to the bible. I was so excited because of my recent adventure, and how much I had learned! I thought this would be a good extension of that study the LORD had led me on. I was excited until the bible study began. I once again found myself in the same spot. Why can't I just enjoy the bible studies', but everything she said was wrong, twisted, and just not right. Which I only knew because of the study that I had just done. Everyone else was so engrossed and loving it, so I demanded of myself that I find the positive things this had to offer. Once again, all I could think was how it felt like she had only read a sentence from all the books I had read, and did not understand it in a real way. It seemed as if she only understood in a superficial way, as if she only read the cliff notes. She would say a lot of true things, but then throw in one part that led the whole subject down the wrong path, making it a false teaching. I could only think how she had no true understanding and was telling people wrong. She even recalled an event that she claimed that she experienced, but I knew that to be from one of the books that I had read. I knew this to be an older book, and there was not any chance that that author stole this from her. I sat there and prayed for GOD's help, when the HOLY SPIRIT told me she had a spirit of deceit on her. In that one moment, all of the pieces snapped together instantaneously. All this time, my flesh was responding to what my spirit was telling me, but I did not have the understanding of it yet. Once I understood why my flesh was reacting that way, it stopped, and my flesh and spirit were on the same page. My mind was then able to snap everything into straight pieces, and untangle it from the snarled ball of fishing line that it was in. (1 John 4)

I sat there just praying and asking GOD for discernment. I could strongly feel this spirit of deceit on her every time we watched her video, or read parts of her book. Though, I also felt peace, and all that other was gone. Discernment and understanding was the piece I was missing. When it all snapped into place, all the confusion and misinterpretation from my mind, of what my spirit was telling me, was gone. Things started to become more clear, as I realized I had always been able to hear people's opinions and really listen, whether I agreed or not, just like at church. But, when the spirit of deceit was entangled, it would hit my spirit wrong. This began a journey of GOD showing me the spirit of deceit and how it's ugly hand is in every type of community, but especially the Christian community.

It seemed, my opinion only, it started with a culture where we do not say 'I do not know' anymore, but instead a culture where we feel like we have to have an opinion, despite not actually knowing anything about it. Then it was coupled with drops of deceit and that mix was a bad recipe. We now have a culture of "know it all's" who know nothing. I was watching a debate on good 'ole Facebook today where people were arguing over the bible, and I found it funny that one of the persons that was arguing, said they had not read the bible really, but formed an opinion anyways on it vs. someone who had read it.

I was reading the bible one day and it talked about how to count your days and make them mean something. Kind of like count your money and make that go somewhere, and not just having nothing to show for it. There was wisdom in that. I then walked by a sweatshirt a day or two later that said ' Count your blessings and not your days'. Immediately I felt the HOLY SPIRIT tell me see? This is what I am teaching you. It sounded good, it sounded positive, but it was the exact opposite of what the bible says. This enemy makes deceit look and seem good, sound positive, but if we do not have a relationship instead of a religion, if we do not know the Word, then we will not have true understanding. We will sway with every wind that comes along with a new or different school of thought. I hear pastors preach, writers write, speakers speak, and deception has settled in, like it is in a comfy couch and has pulled out the recliner, ready for a long stay. The scripture that comes to my mind is be aware of the snakes, but in this case, the snake is the spirit of deceit, and it has entered into our Christian community. (Matthew 10:16).

I have watched the spirit of deceit create a base for which this world is going to build on for the end of times to become normal and common. If the Christian community is too busy being confused along with the rest of the world, then what light are we shining? I read a book from my old pastor, whom I loved his sermons, and he said we should go back to the days where people were outraged and nailed pages from the bible on the church's doors. I recently heard a sermon solely on physical laziness, and I thought the irony of that sermon. For several days in my prayer time, I kept seeing this huge black net over the churches. I could not understand why I kept seeing this and feeling it for days, but I could feel the message the HOLY SPIRIT was telling me. The enemy is laying a net of deceit over the churches and whispering SSSHHHHH to the churches, and the church is listening. The enemy is laying over a net wanting to churches to be quiet on what he is doing, and we are complying.

Any time GOD tells me something, HE confirms it everywhere; with people, the bible, using whatever, wherever. The next month, I was surrounded by people having the same message. Several people that I know, were telling me GOD was telling them to get ready. The Christians are about to be tested in this world. I do not really know who Glenn Beck is, but I somehow came across a video of him telling of his dream on this. I immediately felt a confirmation from the HOLY SPIRIT. Other people that I knew were being told to get their house in order. Testimony after testimony, it was all the same message from GOD, on how the real Christians are about to be separated from the one who say they are. I began to question why HE didn't tell me and I started to take this personally!

I'm not quite sure where this will lead, but I do believe that the spirit of deception has woven it's way into the Christian community from every angle, and we ate the good looking fruit core and all. Then those seeds have planted themselves into us, and we have internalized the lies, watered it, gave it soil, and it has grown out of control. The spirit of deception has whispered into the ears and made a foundation of lies. It uses positive words that sound good, but do not have any substance, and in the end only lead to death. The only way to combat this, is to be in GOD's word, pray, fast, and seek HIM in all things. (1 Timothy 4:1, 2 timothy 4:3-4) Let us pray that GOD reveal truth and remove the enemies' deceptions from us! This reminds me of Revelations, where JESUS is telling each church where its strengths and weaknesses are. We need to be asking GOD where we are weak and blindsided by the enemy, so we can overcome and be the light that GOD has called us to be!

If you like this article, I have also written:
GOD'S Love, and GOD in My Fire.

My name is Jemael Partlow. I am a traveling CST and I have been married for 25 years. We have three grown amazing kids! I enjoy the outdoors. I hike, kayak, hunt, on a paintball team, and enjoy a good campfire. I also love exploring GOD'S word and learning all about it! I hold a small annual conference where speakers, including myself, tell our testimonies. I am also currently writing a book about the end times, which I've studied off and on for two years. I'm excited about this new project, while I still have my small support group for moms and or wives who have children or spouses who have mental health issues. I am also a Christian certified mentor, which I truly enjoy doing!

DEBBIE COLE

MARY HAD A LITTLE LAMB
.(Excerpted from her book, *Am I a Sheep?!?!)*

Lambs can hardly keep their feet on the ground! They are full of joy, leaping and jumping. Oh, that I would be as expressive of my joy every day. No matter what. Like Jesus taught, we need to see the Father's world with wide eyes and open minds. To seek Him as a child seeks its Mommy and Daddy. To appreciate the joy of life and to seek the joy of heaven.

That's why He commanded parents to: "Love the LORD your God with all your heart and with all your soul and with all your strength. [6]These commandments that I give you today are to be upon your hearts. [7]**Impress them on your children**" (Deut. 6:5-7a NIV) *emphasis mine*.

As a Child

Jesus made it clear that the children, all children, are wanted. All are loved by Him and the Father. One of my favorite memories of this lesson was taught by a Deaf preacher. When I was a little girl, my parents served as sign language interpreters for the Deaf ministry at Columbus Avenue Church of Christ in Waco. Twice a month they would hold separate worship services for the Deaf. The Deaf evangelist would come preach so they could "hear" the message in their own language. One Sunday morning, I was sitting at the front during the service while he was preaching. He read the following verses in Luke.

People were also bringing babies to Jesus to have him touch them. When the disciples saw this, they rebuked them. [16]But Jesus called the children to him and said, "Let the little children come to me, and do not hinder them, for the kingdom of God belongs to such as these. ¹⁷I tell you the truth, anyone who will not receive the kingdom of God like a little child will never enter it" (Luke 18:15-17 NIV).

Then he read the following passage from Matthew:

At that time the disciples came to Jesus and asked, "Who is the greatest in the kingdom of heaven?" ²He called a little child and had him stand among them. ³And he said: "I tell you the truth, unless you change and become like little children, you will never enter the kingdom of heaven. ⁴Therefore whoever humbles himself like this child is the greatest in the kingdom of heaven. ⁵And whoever welcomes a little child like this in my name welcomes me" (Matt. 18:1-5 NIV).

At that point, the Deaf preacher reached down and took my hand so I would get up and stand beside him. Then with one hand on my shoulder, he went on preaching to illustrate the verses just read. I'll never forget it. He said in sign language, "Jesus loves this child. Jesus wants this child. Jesus has called this child and God has chosen her." Then he smiled at me and sent me back to my seat. I'm not sure exactly how old I was. It couldn't have been more than ten. But the message that day spoke volumes to me. Maybe that is why I can so easily visualize God saying that to me with His hand on my shoulder. God gifted me to later become an interpreter serving my Deaf brothers and sisters in Christ. I am chosen. I am loved. And so are you, dear friend.

Lambing season is full of excitement, anticipation and sometimes loss. Most lambs are born without any assistance, and shortly after they've hit the ground they are standing wobbly, searching for the ewe's teat. Once they begin suckling their tails spin like propellers. Almost 20 percent of lambs die before weaning; 80 percent of those die during the first ten days of life. Keeping them alive and healthy is a real challenge. It is vital that a lamb stands on its own and begin nursing within an hour of birth. If necessary, a ewe will paw the ground around a lamb to get it up. Then nuzzle it toward the nipple repeatedly until the lamb nurses.

As lambs grow, getting taller, it becomes necessary for them to be on their knees to nurse until they are weaned. What a beautiful thought that as we mature, we too need to be on our knees to receive the life-sustaining communion with the LORD. This humble position helps us to see that we are solely dependent on God and His blessings to nourish our souls. When we kneel and pray His scriptures back to Him, we are feeding the spirit and satisfying the soul.

At nap time, lambs seek out their mothers and sleep as close to them as they can. Healthy lambs sleep eight to twelve hours daily. Lambs, like children, need to grow and mature to adult sheep. As lambs they are vulnerable to all the external forces around them. Sheep, too, face those externals, but they know the shepherd and that makes them different. I felt it would be beneficial to identify some of the key idiosyncrasies between lambs and sheep.

Lambs Compared to Sheep

Fearful or Trusting

In comparing lambs to sheep, lambs are fearful of the shepherd. Sheep look to the shepherd. Lambs panic and run for fear of the unknown. Their fear causes them to do dangerous things, such as crash into fences. When lambs are newborn, it is beneficial to spray iodine on their navels to disinfect and promote healing, because they will be lying next to Mom in the dirt, the grass, and trampled hay, etc. When you enter the pen or pasture to spray them, the lambs immediately run, hide and bleat for Mom, while the ewes simply note you are there and continue whatever they were doing when you came through the gate. Sheep have experienced the shepherd's routine and care. The shepherd's presence is comforting. If the shepherd uses herding dogs, they've become "dog broke." In other words, they are habituated to the shepherd sending a dog to gather them. They know there is no danger. The shepherd is waiting.

Marshmallow's Run at the Gate

One day I was sorting out sheep from the flock to practice herding with the dog. A lamb (Marshmallow) got separated from his mama and I couldn't get him to leave the sheep I was sorting to go back to Mom. Finally, I was able to move the sheep I needed into a smaller pen and close the gate before the lamb ran in. As I was walking toward the other gate, *which was standing wide open,* to have the lamb join mama and the flock, he turned and ran back, headlong into the gate with the sorted sheep. In the process, he broke his horn and it was bleeding.

Now more than ever, I needed to get him back with the flock so I could put some wound heal spray on the horn. He was leaping and running behind the rest of the flock. I finally had to straddle him and hold his neck with one arm, while spraying the horn with the other. He bellowed the entire time, which was just minutes, not the hour he imagined it to be.

"There is a way that seems right to a man, but in the end it leads to death" (Pr. 14:12 NIV). That little lamb was fortunate that he only broke his horn. I've seen adult sheep do the same thing and break their necks. He was so sure he knew the way to get back with his mama and the flock that he was willing to risk everything on a whim because he didn't want to follow the shepherd. How often we find ourselves in similar circumstances. God is leading us one way. The door is closed our way, but another gate is standing open. Yet, we run kicking and screaming in the opposite direction. We cannot see God's wisdom or His plan for us. Sometimes the lesson learned is painful and we are bloodied. LORD willing, we will submit, or we will die.

Dependent or Interdependent

Lambs in general are very dependent on their mothers, clinging closely to them and nursing at will until they are removed for weaning. Mature sheep have learned the value of sticking together and moving as one. A sheep separated from the flock becomes agitated and stressed. They know they need each other.

Wandering or Settled

Lambs are full of wanderlust until about four months old. They spend less and less time with Mom and more time checking out their surroundings. It's like something is calling them out of the safety of the flock and away from Mom, toward who knows what. They get stuck in fences or escape and get lost. Sheep know their home pasture. Where to find shade, water and which gates will open. Those on open fields with natural boundaries of creeks, mountains, and foothills become "heft" to their pasture. Consequently, the flock will not wander as a group from their usual grazing areas.

Playful or Curious

Lambs are very active when they are healthy. They play together. Lambs love to climb! They love to run, and jump for joy in their play. I've seen lambs jump on the back of a resting ram, then jump off again and again and again. As they get older, they play king of the hill on the tall round hay bales. Sheep are very curious. Do something in the pasture for the first time and all eyes are on you. I've been working my border collie, Junebug, in a large field with a few sheep, only to look up and see all of those in the pen lined up along the fence, watching every move we make.

David had the opportunity to the see the joy of lambs. He witnessed the playfulness of sheep. He writes in the Psalms: "The LORD is my strength and my shield; my heart trusts in him, and I am helped. My heart leaps for joy and I will give thanks to him in song" (Ps. 28:7 NIV). And "The mountains skipped like rams, the hills like lambs. …[6]you mountains, that you skipped like rams, you hills, like lambs?" (Ps. 114:4, 6 NIV) refers to the joy of creation in the presence of the LORD as God made the Jordan River part for the Israelites. I believe that we too should leap for joy before the LORD, like David did, when he returned the ark to Jerusalem.

Scatter or Flock

Lambs without their mothers tend to be more flighty and will readily disperse rather than stick with the group or flock. Sheep are aware of each other in the field or pasture no matter how big it is, and will readily come together to graze, rest or chew their cud. I've seen the flock out grazing, spread over the pasture. Then all at once, as if someone rang a dinner bell, they all start moving toward each other and together as they move to the water, to the barnyard or up the hill.

Seeking or Following

Lambs are naturally curious about their environment, which can get them into trouble if risks are present. As they grow older, they spend less time with Mom and more with the other lambs. Sheep look to their established leaders for guidance. If the leader is moving, they are following. It tends to be an old ewe leading the flock. It's their tendency to follow that makes it possible for a shepherd to lead them no matter the size of the flock. In our case, we need to be open to our Shepherd's direction. Furthermore, we like the sheep need to be willing to follow. Have you seen large flocks of sheep following the shepherd? There may be hundreds strung out in a line for a mile or more, and yet they follow.

Demanding or Waiting

A lamb separated from its mother, because it wasn't paying attention when she moved, or on the wrong side of the gate, will bleat for Mom to come. The ewe will generally turn and call the lamb toward her. If the lamb's bleat turns to panic, she'll run toward the lamb, calling all the way. After the lambs are pulled from their mothers for weaning, they will bleat and call for Mama incessantly for two or three days. Finally, they will give up since it is obvious that Mama and her comfort are nowhere in sight. It becomes out of sight, out of mind. *It should be noted that the ewes also grieve the loss of their lamb. They call for them as well.*

There was a hard lambing season at Crystal Valley where I kept my sheep. The sheep rancher had a ewe with twins, and one died for no apparent reason twenty-four hours after birth. The mother ewe, with her remaining lamb in tow, searched, calling all over the place for the lost lamb for more than a day. It was heart-wrenching to see and hear.

There are periods in my life when, for whatever reason, I need God desperately and want His presence. Unlike the mama ewes, my God is always there, and He hears my every call. Greater still, He answers me. Meditate on this verse: "Before they call I will answer; while they are still speaking I will hear" (Is. 65:24 NIV). I love that promise! God knows exactly where I am. He knows what I'm feeling, and He provides for me.

Like the lambs, waiting brings impatience. I want my needs met. I can't stand it any longer! God and I have had many a discussion about this flaw in my character over the years. I have always felt that He had a higher opinion of my ability to handle adversity and to wait than I did. In times of crises, I didn't know what to pray for, or, thankfully, anything I could do to make a difference. I simply had to wait. No matter how much I cried, everything would be done in His time.

In all my years of following God, He has never let me down. He has certainly left me waiting, however. But He is always just a prayer away. In 1 Samuel 13, Saul waited at Gilgal for Samuel to arrive and offer the sacrifices. He waited a week and Samuel hadn't arrived yet. Worse, people were leaving. So, Saul decided to offer the sacrifices himself. No sooner had he done it, Samuel arrived, asking, "What have you done?" Notice Saul's response (*I'm paraphrasing*): "I waited a week; people were leaving, and you didn't come!" But Samuel did come, in God's time.

Sheep will generally tend to stand and wait for you to open a gate, to break the ice off the water trough, to tag and band the lambs. However, if they are hungry and you are coming to feed, they too will bleat until they are fed. No matter the season, they must wait on the shepherd. Sometimes, it is because they have gotten themselves into trouble, caught in a fence, or stuck in the mire. Other times they are under examination because of injury or disease. During the drought, they may be hungry for green grass and forage, but they have to rely on the shepherd providing hay and grain. No matter the circumstance, the shepherd will come provide for their needs -- but in his time.

Throughout my Christian life, God has given me multiple opportunities to wait on Him. I could do nothing to help or speed up the process. I simply had to wait, trusting God would see me through. Waiting was actually easier this time. To just be still and know He is God. You see, in playing with the sheep, I gained a whole new perspective on my relationship with God. I knew He knew the future. He knows the past and the present. He knows me inside and out. Furthermore, He knows what I can bear with His strength. He knows exactly what I need.

That seemed to baffle some folks. But you know, I always told my co-workers, my staff, my interpreters, my friends and my family that God will take care of it, whatever the problem is. I've also prayed with and requested prayers from all of those mentioned above, confident He would answer. So, as I sat in His waiting room, I felt that my experience was not only for me but for those watching. For them to know my trust in my God and my Shepherd is more than talk. It was tested! My hope is that God is pleased with my progress on this journey through life – at least in recent months. Knowing that whatever the outcome, God is God and I am His.

Careless or Careful

A lamb will let its curiosity lead it toward a dog and stand there watching to see what the dog will do. In the case of a sheep dog, the lamb will learn to respect the dog, but will not be injured in the process. However, this curiosity can lead it toward a predator. In fear, a lamb will blindly run away from the flock, making it more vulnerable. Sometimes it runs right into the jaws of a cunning fox or coyote. So, why do we need a shepherd? By God's grace and His alone, we have the opportunity to learn from our mistakes and be rescued in the process.

Sheep are always aware of their surroundings. Leaders will be careful to look up and scan the surroundings while in the field, as they graze close together. They are more able to stave off wolf attacks using their group size to their advantage.

It Takes a Flock

As Christians, we've learned the importance of a support group, **the Church**, to look out for each other. We hold each other accountable. We depend on those God has surrounded us with as we live daily in His presence. Once, I went out to check on my new lambs. The flock was out in the pasture when I arrived. As I entered the gate to the pen where we feed, they saw me and came up. In the process, three brand new lambs ended up on the wrong side of the gate. They couldn't figure out how to get to the group, even though the gate was standing open. The lambs started bleating for help. Immediately, not only the mamas but the entire flock went running down to the fence to comfort the lambs and call them to them. Standing next to Mama with a fence between them, they stopped bleating. So, the flock headed back up toward me and the feed troughs. When the mamas turned toward the flock, the lambs bellowed again. This time the flock not only moved toward them, but the old ewe leading the group led them through the gate and past it. At that point, the lambs could see the flock with no barriers between them. They quickly scampered toward the flock. Once everyone was together, the lead sheep headed the flock back up the hill through the gate.

What a perfect example! You see, we too sometimes find ourselves in the wrong place or separated from our Christian brothers and sisters. Thankfully, in the family of God, the flock will come to our rescue. Better still, wise leaders will show us the way out or the way back to the safety of the flock. I am continually awed by God's wisdom. He not only draws us to Him, He also sends other believers to rescue us. A perfect plan made with us in mind.

No Tags or Tagged to Belong

In agriculture and pastoral vernacular, a lamb is referred to as a lamb for two years. Although, in their second year they are sometimes called yearlings. Generally, the sheep are there to stay a part of the flock and belong to the shepherd. With lambs, however, it remains to be seen. The shepherd determines if the lamb will become a permanent part of the flock, sold or raised for slaughter. It all depends on the shepherd's plan and purpose. However, the plan can be altered by the lamb in the event it tends to stray. Every member of the flock has a purpose as designated by the shepherd.

Sheep are tagged to identify ownership. Tagging is done to lambs within weeks of their birth. *Note: Lambs going to the sale barn or slaughterhouse can be tagged just prior to going into the auction arena.* In the case of "meat" sheep, premise tags are required to identify not only the owner but the farm/ranch they are from.

The tag is attached to either ear, toward the center or on the edge. The color of the tag and the owner's name serve as a branding mark. The lambs are also banded to dock the tails and neuter ram lambs. Docking of the tails helps with hygiene. Muck doesn't get trapped on the tail or caked on the anus. Ram lambs are generally neutered by banding to prevent inbreeding if they remain with the flock. The shepherd usually takes this opportunity to give vaccines or wormer before they are released back to the flock.

The process requires each individual lamb to be pulled from the flock and its mama. The lamb is scared and wiggling to get free. Once the tagging is complete, they lie down by their mamas, writhing in pain. It takes about thirty minutes for the band to make the tail or scrotum go numb. I am sure they see it as harsh and cruel, but it is a very necessary part of life for a sheep. We too have experiences where we don't know why something is happening. We just know it hurts. Our Shepherd knows our pain and suffering first-hand. He is always there to comfort and heal us. Moreover, He claims us as His own and puts His stamp on us. "Then I looked, and there before me was the Lamb, standing on Mount Zion, and with him 144,000 who had his name and his Father's name written on their foreheads" (Rev. 14:1 NIV).

Milk or "Meat" *grass and grain*

This contrast between lambs and sheep, I will elaborate on more in the next chapter. This can make the difference between life and death: physically for the lambs, and spiritually for us.

Here is the list of differences described in more detail in the previous pages. Is there anything in this comparison that really stands out? If so, what is it? In looking at the list, are you more like a sheep or are there lingering lamb traits?

Lambs	**Sheep**
Fearful	Trusting
Dependent	Interdependent
Wander	Settled
Playful	Curious
Scatter	Flock
Seeking	Following
Demanding	Waiting
Careless	Careful
No Tags	Tagged to belong
Milk	Meat" *Grass, Grain*

We are in the midst of the Christmas season as I write this chapter. Amid all the Christmas decorations around the city there are numerous nativity scenes displayed. All different sizes and styles with one commonality, baby Jesus in the manger. I am thrilled that during this season, people all over the world are stopping to celebrate the birth of our Savior and our Shepherd. Yes, Mary bore a little lamb, Jesus. He came to save the world. Greater news...the incarnate Son of God did not remain a baby. He grew up! He lived and experienced life as we do with all of the pain, joy, and sorrows. He fulfilled God's law. He provided the perfect example of how to live on this earth. He showed us the way to the Father.

During lambing season, sometimes a ewe will reject her lamb. Or die during the birth process, leaving the lamb as an orphan. Another ewe will not accept the lamb even if she has a stillborn lamb and plenty of milk. Shepherds will take the blood of the ewe from the afterbirth, or better still blood from the dead lamb, and rub it all over the orphan. Now the ewe only smells the blood and recognizes it as hers. Then she will accept the blood-covered orphan as her own.

It is the same with us. We are separated from God because of our sin. Our holy God cannot accept sin, and therefore rejects us. But the redeeming blood of Jesus covers us and washes away our sin. "This is how we know what love is: Jesus Christ laid down his life for us" (1 John 3:16 NIV). Then when God looks at us, He sees the blood of His Son and accepts us as His own. "But now in Christ Jesus you who once were far away have been brought near through the blood of Christ" (Eph. 2:13 NIV). We receive the cleansing blood when we put on Christ in baptism for the remission of our sins.

The Good News....In His death on the cross, He became the sacrificial lamb for all our sins. He died and rose again, to bring salvation and life eternal for all who follow Him! As the Apostle Peter preached on the Day of Pentecost:

"Therefore let all Israel be assured of this: God has made this Jesus, whom you crucified, both Lord and Christ." [37]When the people heard this, they were cut to the heart and said to Peter and the other apostles, "Brothers, what shall we do?" [38]Peter replied, "Repent and be baptized, every one of you, in the name of Jesus Christ for the forgiveness of your sins. And you will receive the gift of the Holy Spirit. [39]The promise is for you and your children and for all who are far off – for all whom the Lord our God will call" (Acts 2:36-39 NIV).

Now as our Shepherd, Jesus stands at the gate, calling us out one by one. Be thankful for His sacrifice. More importantly, follow Him wherever He leads you.

Questions to Ponder

1. Do you experience joy and wonder in being alive in the Father's world? Can those around you see your joy?

2. Have you had an experience like Marshmallow, wanting the closed gate to be open to you? What did it take to come to your senses?

3. What stands out to you in the differences between lambs and sheep? Which list is more definitive of your relationship or life with God? He's ready and willing to help you grow. Will you let Him?

Author Biography

I am a wife, mother, and grandmother that has been working as a sign language interpreter in various settings since 1984. I grew up in the church, a baptized believer following Jesus. But my eyes were opened and my relationship to God was deepened in 2012. That year, I was introduced to sheep up close because I was training to become a handler of sheep herding dogs. I bought my own sheep to practice with the dogs. God used those sheep and my sheepdogs to help me understand the relationship between sheep and their shepherd but more importantly my relationship to God Himself and the Good Shepherd, Jesus. One on one in the sheep fields I spent time with the Father and my Shepherd, my relationship grew to a whole new level. In the 21st century we are so far removed from the pastoral setting of the Bible; it is often difficult to relate to the stories and parables in the Bible. My prayer is that knowledge of the sheep and shepherd relationship will help you to deepen your relationship to God.

Website: iamasheep.net

Published works include:

I Am A Sheep?!?!

Made For A Purpose: Lessons From My Sheepdogs

Sign Language and the Health Care Professional

All are available on Amazon.

BRIDGET THOMAS

ONE PRAYER AT A TIME

"Everyone has problems," my husband said into the phone. He was talking to his sister and sharing some of the troubles that we had been dealing with. And my sister-in-law also shared some of the things that her family was facing.

We all do have different problems on different levels. Some seasons of our lives feel harder to bear than others. Some days feel hopeless. Some days our faith waivers. Some days we are weak with the weight of our worries.

However, it doesn't have to be this way. Yes, there will always be problems on this earth. Yet we don't have to lose our hope or our faith.

But this begs the question - how do we make it through? You have heard of the saying "one day at a time." I am adopting a different spin on that - "One Prayer at a Time." That is the key to surviving through tough times.

One thing I have discovered is that in troubled times we have a choice. Problems can either tear us down, or we can choose to draw closer to God. We can choose to cling to Him in prayer. We can choose to trust Him.

I know it's not always easy, especially because it seems like when it rains it pours. Many times, it's not just one problem we are dealing with, but several. When we are bombarded with various troubles, we might feel as though we can't keep our heads above the water that is pouring down.

That's when we choose to stop fighting the waves and surrender into the arms of the Lord. He is our lifeline. According to Oxford, a lifeline is "a thing on which someone or something depends or which provides a means of escape from a difficult situation." That is exactly what God can be for us during difficult times. But we have to make that choice to draw near to Him. And I have found that prayer is vital to stay afloat.

Prayer brings us comfort during difficulties. Throughout any given day we will face tasks that we don't want to deal with, bumps that suddenly arise in the road, unexpected situations that come our way, and more. So how can we survive when we feel like we're walking through a landmine? One prayer at a time.

In 1 Thessalonians 5:17 it says to "pray continually." Some Bible translations say to "pray without ceasing." We might wonder - how do we pray without ceasing? That seems like an impossible task. But I have found that talking with God all throughout the day, and praying for strength and guidance in each situation – this brings peace in the midst of the storm. This echoes what Paul told us in Philippians 4:6-7: "Do not be anxious about anything, but in every situation, by prayer and petition, with thanksgiving, present your requests to God. And the peace of God, which transcends all understanding, will guard your hearts and your minds in Christ Jesus."

And something that amazes me is how God is always there, ready to listen to our every word. When I was a child, my maternal grandparents lived over a thousand miles away. When I was very young, my grandfather passed away. At the time, my mother traveled to be with my grandmother and spent a few months with her. Returning home worried my mother because she felt as though she was leaving my grandmother all alone, far away from everyone.

This prompted my mother and grandmother to start a new routine. This was when everyone had landlines and mobile phones were unheard of. Every single night before heading to bed one of them would ring the other one's phone and hang up. Then the recipient of the initial ring would ring back and hang up. Some nights my grandmother got to it first, so she would ring and hang up. My mother would then dial my grandmother, let her phone ring a couple of times, and hang up. Other nights my mother might have gotten to it first, so the order was reversed. Of course, if one of them felt like talking that night, then they would answer the phone, let the phone keep ringing, or maybe even call back. But the majority of nights, they would ring and hang up.

This went on for around fifteen years, until it was time for my grandmother to live with my mother. The ring each night was a message letting my mother know that my grandmother was safe, she was okay, and all was well. And it also gave my grandmother a way to connect with someone each evening, since she lived alone at the time. The ring of the phone provided a sense of comfort to both parties. The ring of the phone was all they needed to go to bed each night in peace.

We too can have comfort and peace every day and every night of our lives. We don't have to ring someone like my mother and grandmother did. We can turn to Jesus in prayer. No matter how alone we might feel at times, we can feel connected to our Lord and Savior every single day. No matter what is weighing on our minds, we can rest assured knowing that He is there. We can connect with Him at any given time.

We don't have to wait to see if God will ring back or answer the phone. He will always be there. And He always hears us when we call on Him. Sometimes it might feel as though God is not listening, but that is never true.

I love reading in the Psalms. They bring me comfort and joy. And I am especially intrigued when I see a theme in the words. When reading through the Psalms in 2020, during a time when the whole world was anxious from the pandemic, I was amazed at how many verses I found that assured me that God hears us when we call. I would like to share some of those verses with you.

- "Know that the LORD has set apart his faithful servant for himself; the LORD hears when I call to him." - Psalm 4:3
- "In the morning, LORD, you hear my voice; in the morning I lay my requests before you and wait expectantly." - Psalm 5:3
- "You, LORD, hear the desire of the afflicted; you encourage them, and you listen to their cry." - Psalm 10:17
- "I call on you, my God, for you will answer me; turn your ear to me and hear my prayer." - Psalm 17:6
- "In my distress I called to the LORD; I cried to my God for help. From his temple he heard my voice; my cry came before him, into his ears." - Psalm 18:6
- "I sought the LORD, and he answered me; he delivered me from all my fears." - Psalm 34:4
- "I waited patiently for the LORD; he turned to me and heard my cry." - Psalm 40:1
- "You who answer prayer, to you all people will come." - Psalm 65:2
- "You answer us with awesome and righteous deeds, God our Savior, the hope of all the ends of the earth and of the farthest seas." - Psalm 65:5
- "But God has surely listened and has heard my prayer." - Psalm 66:19
- "The LORD hears the needy and does not despise his captive people." - Psalm 69:33
- "When I am in distress, I call to you, because you answer me." - Psalm 86:7
- "I love the LORD, for he heard my voice; he heard my cry for mercy." - Psalm 116:1

- "I call on the LORD in my distress, and he answers me." - Psalm 120:1
- "When I called, you answered me; you greatly emboldened me." - Psalm 138:3
- "The LORD is near to all who call on him, to all who call on him in truth." - Psalm 145:18
- "He fulfills the desires of those who fear him; he hears their cry and saves them." - Psalm 145:19

These are just a few promises found in the Bible, which tell us that God hears us, He is there when we call, and He answers us. If we cry out to Him, pray to Him, praise Him or even just whisper to Him - He always hears the voices of His children. And more than that, He answers. What a wonderful gift we have in prayer.

I mentioned that I love reading the Psalms. I also love reading the Gospels. Not only do they provide us with an inside look at our Savior, but they also show us how we are to live when we follow Him. One theme I have seen in the life of Jesus was how much time He spent in prayer. Luke 5:16 is one example where it says, "But Jesus often withdrew to lonely places and prayed." When I read verses like this, I have to wonder - if this time alone with the Father was vital for Jesus, how much more important should it be for us?

I admit that when I was a young Christian, I didn't put enough weight in prayer life. Thankfully, as I have grown closer to the Lord, He has shown me how valuable prayer is. I see now that prayer is so much more than something we check off of our to do lists. Prayer is not something we *have* to do; prayer is something we *get* to do. Prayer is an honor and a privilege. We are able to meet with our loving Father at any time and from anywhere.

And something that astonishes me is that I can see how in prayer I am being shaped and formed to be more like Jesus. We are molded into the person God purposed us to be when we meet with Him in prayer. Prayer helps us to shed the gunk of this world as we are transformed from the inside out. Whether we are crying out in despair, whispering words of gratitude, calling out in praise, or begging for divine help - He is there. He is eager to hear from us. He listens to every word. And He is happy to help us and wrap us in His loving arms.

Spending time with God in prayer also helps us to learn more about Him. We begin to understand how incredibly merciful and faithful He is. We are filled with awe at His goodness. His love fills a void deep within our hearts.

When we sit in God's presence and have a conversation with Him, we are forming a strong bond and a meaningful relationship. God is incredibly fond of us and longs to hear from us. Through prayer we not only receive strength, help and guidance, but we also receive love and tender care. May we remember the priceless gift we have in prayer.

I may not know what you are facing today. I may not know what you have been dealing with in this season of your life. But one thing I do know is that God is only a prayer away. He is there for you. He is ready and waiting for you to call upon Him. He loves you beyond measure. And He wants you to reach out to Him. And He will hear every word. He will get you through whatever you are facing – one prayer at a time.

Dear Heavenly Father, I admit that stress has been bringing me down. But I turn to You in prayer, today and every day. You alone can help me. You give me strength, hope, and courage. I put my trust in You. I hold onto the words in Psalm 118: 6 - "The Lord is with me" (NIV), "The Lord is for me" (NLT), "The Lord is on my side" (NKJV). What comfort those words bring. Thank You for always being there for me. Thank you for always hearing my prayers. I hand all my stress over to You. I know this doesn't mean I will never have any problems. But it does mean I can lean on You through it all. Thank You, God. I am so thankful for You. I praise Your Holy Name and I love You. In Jesus' beautiful name I pray, Amen.

Author Biography:

Bridget A. Thomas is the author of *Every Day is a Gift*, You Are Redeemed, and Giving God Your Whole Heart. She lives in Florida with her husband and two furbabies. Her obsessions are Jesus, books, and coffee. Bridget and her husband enjoy watching baseball games and traveling to the Smoky Mountains. To learn more about Bridget, visit her at bridgetathomas.com.

Every Day is a Gift!
Bridget

BRIDGET THOMAS

A SECRET LIFE

What if I told you I knew the secret to life? I have found that there are two easy practices we can incorporate into our daily lives to make each day filled with joy. Even when we are walking through something difficult, we can still find contentment. No matter what life throws at us, we can have peace.

And what are these two practices? Praise and gratitude. These two habits can transform our hearts, our outlook, and our lives. Praise and gratitude go hand-in-hand because our praise increases our gratitude and our gratitude increases our praise.

Why are praise and gratitude so powerful?

- God is in the midst of our praises. Have you ever heard the saying that "God inhabits the praise of His people?" That comes from Psalm 22:3 in which the King James Version says, "But thou art holy, O thou that inhabitest the praises of Israel." Praising God draws us closer to Him and helps us to feel His presence.

- The enemy hates our praises, so he runs in the other direction. It is believed that before his fall, the enemy played a big part in the heavenly music (see Ezekiel 28:13). But his pride got the better of him and he wanted to be exalted (see Isaiah 14:12-15). Therefore, it makes sense that he wouldn't like hearing the songs we sing to the Lord.

- Praise and gratitude take our attention off of any issues we might be facing. The more we focus on our problems, the bigger they seem to become.

- Praise and gratitude turn our eyes towards God. When we focus on Him and how amazing He is, our troubles seem to shrink in comparison to His greatness. I like how Psalm 69:30 (ESV) says, "I will praise the name of God with a song; I will magnify him with thanksgiving."
- We remember God's faithfulness during good times and not-so-good times.
- Praise and gratitude help us to see that the Lord is our source and our strength. When we have Jesus, we have enough. He is all we need. And as our Good Shepherd, He will provide for us.
- Praise and gratitude remind us that we don't have to worry and fret because we have the Most High God by our side.
- When we are intentional about looking for the good in our lives and giving God thanks for the blessings, it can change our hearts.
- Praise and gratitude supernaturally lift our spirits. Our hearts pour out to God, and He in turn fills our hearts.

Praise and gratitude are habits that we should incorporate into our lives, no matter what is going on around us. We might be more inclined to give thanks and praise God when things are going well. However, even when circumstances in our lives aren't going well - that is when we need to praise God and give thanks the most! I know it might seem difficult to get started when our feelings aren't in it. However, once we begin, our hearts and mood will turn around.

I have seen this firsthand in my own life. One example happened on a Monday morning a while back. My husband had to tend to some important banking matters that day. I wanted to ask my boss if I could take a couple of hours off so my husband and I could handle it together. However, I also had a big meeting that day, which I couldn't miss. And this big meeting was also an added stressor, so there were two things weighing on my mind that morning. I was anxious and fretful.

As I drove to work, I decided to praise and give thanks to the Lord. Then something miraculous happened. I felt peace settle over me. I was no longer worried about the big things my husband and I were facing that day. I knew God was in control and He would help us through them. And He did! Everything turned out well with both situations.

Another example happened on a day when I was working remotely and I had to get an important task completed by the end of the day. However, my internet went down around lunch time. I used my phone to check with the company and saw that they knew of an outage and they were working on it. Since it was around noon, I decided to take a lunch break while the company worked on the issue. Later the internet came back up and I got back to work. Or so I thought. The internet seemed to sporadically go down here and there for the next couple of hours. Each time I checked my internet provider's website, they had a new time on when they estimated the issues would be resolved. I was so frustrated!

Sometimes things like this are spiritual attacks from the enemy. And that is how I felt about this situation. Therefore, I prayed about it. Then I thanked God for being in control and for handling the problem. And after that I put praise music on my phone and sang along with the songs. After taking these steps, things turned around. My internet issues improved, I was able to complete the project I was working on, and most of all I felt so much better. My frustration turned to joy and peace.

I could share more personal stories that reveal the importance of praise and gratitude, but instead I would like to share a biblical story.

David was a great example of someone in the Bible who praised the Lord often. There is one particular story concerning David which illustrates the importance of praising God, and the consequences of not praising God.

In 2 Samuel 6, we read about David and his men bringing the Ark of the Lord to Jerusalem. David was "rejoicing" (v 12) and "David was dancing before the Lord with all his might, while he and all Israel were bringing up the ark of the Lord with shouts and the sound of trumpets" (v 14-15). This is a beautiful picture of the king of Israel praising the Lord.

However, there is another person in this story who doesn't have the same attitude. David had a wife named Michal. (She was also King Saul's daughter. There was a lot of tension between Saul and David in the latter part of Saul's reign. But that's a story for another time!) Michal "watched from a window. And when she saw King David leaping and dancing before the Lord, she despised him in her heart" (v 16). While picturing David's praise brought something sweet to the story, picturing Michal's disgust brings a sour taste.

And the story doesn't end there. When David arrived at home, Michal told him exactly how she felt. She said, "How the king of Israel has distinguished himself today going around half-naked in full view of the slave girls of his servants as any vulgar fellow would" (v 20). But David didn't back down.

He replied to her, "It was before the Lord, who chose me rather than your father or anyone from his house when he appointed me ruler over the Lord's people Israel – I will celebrate before the Lord. I will become even more undignified than this, and I will be humiliated in my own eyes. But by the slave girls you spoke of, I will be held in honor" (v 21-22).

The worst part of the story is yet to come. In verse 23 it says, "And Michal daughter of Saul had no children to the day of her death." How very sad that the story ended this way for her.

I appreciate that this story is in the Bible, as it is a good reminder of the importance of praising God with our whole heart. David didn't care what other people thought of him. His eyes were on God and His opinion. That is why David was called a man after God's own heart. The Lord wants us to seek Him wholeheartedly. And when we praise Him, He can see and feel our love pouring out.

How can we increase praise and gratitude in our daily lives?

- Personally, I keep a gratitude journal. I write down blessings from each day. It could be something simple like a beautiful sunset, or something bigger like an answered prayer. I have been doing this for years, and I can say that this practice has truly changed my outlook on life.
- Read the Psalms. This book of the Bible is so special to me. During good times and during difficult times, I

have found joy and peace in these words. Use the Psalms as a scavenger hunt, searching for verses that speak of the Lord's love for you. And in turn this will increase your devotion to Him.

- Each morning I write down a verse from the Psalms, and then I also write out a prayer pertaining to that verse. This habit helps me to begin my day with a heart turned towards God.

- Listen to praise music and sing praises. I'm not the best singer, but I don't think God cares about how well we can carry a tune. He just loves to hear our praises. And singing helps us to feel joyful. One day recently I turned on some music and sang along. It had been a while since I'd done this. I used to sing in my car on my commute, but now that I work from home, I've had less music in my life. During this time period, I had some stressful work days and I was feeling down. After a couple of hours of listening to my favorite worship songs, I thought, *I really needed this*! I felt like a new person. It's silly because I know how vital praise is. Yet there are times when we need to remind ourselves of truth.

- Remember the cross. As Christians, we have so much to be thankful for. When we remember the sacrifice that Jesus made on the cross, this helps us to overflow with praise and gratitude. And as the writer of Hebrews said, "Through Jesus, therefore, let us continually offer to God a sacrifice of praise—the fruit of lips that openly profess his name." (Heb 13:15 NIV)

- Talk to God. Simply tell God all that you are grateful for. And praise Him for the awesome and mighty God He is.

- Bonus if you can get outdoors when doing any of these. Being in creation helps us reduce stress, relax, and discover supernatural contentment.

Those are a few practical ways that I incorporate praise and gratitude into my life. And I encourage you to add to the list by coming up with your own unique ways to express praise and thanksgiving towards the Lord.

Too often in our culture we are trained to see the negative in every situation and in every person. But as Christians, we have the power of the Holy Spirit who can help us break this cycle. Let's be radically different from those around us. Let's look around for the good. God's goodness and blessings are all around us. We can choose how we will face every moment of every day – with praise and gratitude. As it says in Psalm 118:24 (ESV), "This is the day that the LORD has made; let us rejoice and be glad in it."

Author Biography:

Bridget A. Thomas is the author of *Every Day is a Gift*, You Are Redeemed, and Giving God Your Whole Heart. She lives in Florida with her husband and two furbabies. Her obsessions are Jesus, books, and coffee. Bridget and her husband enjoy watching baseball games and traveling to the Smoky Mountains. To learn more about Bridget, visit her at bridgetathomas.com.

Every Day is a Gift!

Bridget

GLORIA PIERRE DEAN

MENDING THE BROKEN

Beverley was ten when on a visit to her Grandma, she did the deed. On the brick floor lay the pieces of the beautiful heirloom vase.

"Oh Beverley," mother cried "not that vase". Amazed and surprised, she remembers that terror filled her young soul. She had broken a family heirloom that she had been told never to touch. Now, it lay smashed in irregular pieces at her feet.

The family talked of repairing it but they knew that it would never be the same again and the monetary loss was huge.

Years later in her twenties, she still recalled her dastardly deed. She needed to forgive herself.

It all came back in a gallop one day when as a nurse, she stood in the clinical room of an abortion clinic where she worked and saw the parts of an aborted baby in its container.

"Why have I not noticed this living life; this child, before?" she asked herself.

Again and with immense horror it came to her that she had colluded with the destruction of a perfect creation. This fact was compounded when she noted that the baby's heart was still beating, even as it was separated from its body. She also saw that the human flesh continued to twitch, but soon all was still.

She found herself weeping uncontrollably. She had assisted with many abortions and only today did she see.... what needed to be seen.

'What a loss'. She was reminded of the broken vase all over again. She left the job and never returned to the clinic. That day changed her life. She knew in her heart that she needed help because she could not stop weeping.

"No more, No more, Beverley." She vowed a covenant promise to herself and to God and she did something that she had not done in decades.

She repented and prayed, "Father forgive me and forgive us for destroying this baby and so many other babies' lives. Open the eyes of the abortion industry to see the enemy's deception".

Only Jesus could mend this wounding, as He had already done on the cross, she thought to herself.

That night as she lay in bed thinking, she heard an inaudible voice say, "You need help and healing".

"Yes, I do, Lord. I do!" she said audibly. So, she contacted and attended counseling locally, where she was encouraged and enabled to forgive herself, based on Jesus' Word. Soon after, she became involved in a Pro-Life group.

She shared her experiences and the fellow searchers listened, empathized and prayed with each other. One woman, Kitty, invited her to church. At the Living Waters Church, the pastor was preaching on a topic that kept her attention for the duration. That day she went forward and rededicated her life to Jesus.

Pastor Steve preached on Creation. She knew that God created the earth and all that was in it but his emphasis was that human life was sacred to God. Based on his sermon, certain truths were highlighted in her mind.

Such as the fact that many parts of the Bible was about living well, life, procreation and healing, that God created races of people with many different facial features, skin colors and languages. He loved them all. They all express who He is and what He wants His glorious Creation to look like.

He did not create robotic beings.

Incredibly, each body is internally the same. The vital organs that He created in each of his created beings are essentially the same and perform the same functions in well coordinated ways to keep people alive and well. Animals however, are different to humans and yet also uniquely made. The fertile ground that He created, is fertile for growing food is good; unless it has been contaminated.

"All things were made by Him" {John 1:3}

"Before I formed you in the womb, I knew you;" {Jeremiah 1:5a}

As she walked away from the church with Kitty, her mind was whirling, so full of thoughts and images and she was so excited that she couldn't relax.

Weeks later, after praying and thinking, she felt that she should train to be a counselor, so she did. Her desire was to help young couples or single people considering abortion. She also began to write a booklet about her personal experience as a nurse which she entitled ' Mending the Broken', which became a bestseller.

As a counselor, her passion was to help women who were going through the unwanted pregnancy crisis. She knew that many women and girls who were pregnant had been raped. As a nurse in the abortion clinic, she had been privy to that sort of information. Many women came for counseling. Prayer was part of each session. Invitations to accept Christ as Saviour were offered to each woman or girl.

Some women, though, not rape victims, were just not ready to have a baby; so they decided to abort their baby instead of dealing with the new life. Beverley tried never to criticize her clients. For some women, pure terror was how they described the thought of being a single unsupported parent.

So, together with Kitty who was also a counselor, and other like minded local counselors, they generated flyers and created podcasts that showed the women, and the men who sometimes came, how to access the local government services and non-profit agencies that would help them find affordable housing, childcare and support.

Thankfully instead of abortion some chose to have their baby adopted.

A healthy baby in a happy home was the desired outcome.

Together with the other counselors, they were often asked to speak to local churches' youth groups. They focused their talks and seminars on the vitally important decision that Christians should make, which is to remain celibate until they were married. Talks included ways to avoid being drawn in or beguiled by members of the opposite sex and things and places to avoid.

So, how did the childhood pain of a broken vase and the savage clinical cutting apart of a perfect life lead to a ministry in counseling?

As Psalms 23:3 says, "He restores [refreshes] my soul". And after you have suffered a little while, the God of all grace [Who imparts all blessing and favor], Who has called you to His [own] eternal glory in Christ Jesus, will Himself complete and make you what you ought to be. {1 Peter 5 :10} AMP

There is such hope in these promises.

God is the Potter and we are the clay....'we are all the work of your hand.' Isaiah 64:8 {NIV} Clay is broken apart and then 'mended' on a wheel by the expert hands of the potter.

As Beverley often says, God mended and restored me in my brokenness and now I am purposed to help others heal and to make Godly decisions and to choose life!

Gloria Pierre Dean - *God My Rock by Patsy Dean.*

RICHARD CHRISTENSON

THE MAIN THING

Leadership writer Steven Covey once penned some memorable advice that all organizations, including Christ's church, need to hear and heed: "The main thing, is to maintain the main thing, as the main thing."

I believe the "Main Thing" every local church needs to maintain as our main thing was given to us by Jesus Christ when He first commissioned His church.

"Jesus came and said to them, 'All authority in heaven and on earth has been given to me. Go therefore and make disciples of all nations, baptizing them in the name of the Father and of the Son and of the Holy Spirit, teaching them to observe all that I have commanded you. And behold, I am with you always, to the end of the age." Matthew 28:18-20/ESV

Clearly Christ's "Main Thing" was "Go Make Disciples"! He didn't tell His followers to "Go entertain spiritual spectators" or "Go cater to Christian customers" or "Go form Jesus fan clubs".

Once "Disciple Making" is determined to be Christ's main thing, church leadership must next determine what work needs to be accomplished to comprehensively carryout Christ's assignment. I strongly endorse Christian author Bill Hull's description of Christ's disciple making task provided by "The Complete Book of Discipleship". The former Pastor, prolific discipleship writer, and current Talbot School of Theology Professor indicates a comprehensive discipleship plan should include three interrelated elements: Deliverance, Development & Deployment.

Deliverance is the evangelistic element of Christ's commission. Deliverance involves evangelizing those who have not yet made a commitment to accept Jesus as their Savior, and follow Him as their Lord.

All church members need to be actively involved in establishing and developing redemptive relationships with those who are not yet followers of Christ. Church members require training, motivation, encouragement, and support in establishing, and profitably (fruitfully) utilizing redemptive relationships (John 15:8). Through our relationships with family members, friends, associates, neighbors, etc., followers of Christ can most effectively share the love of God, the truth about sin and salvation, the eternal benefits of becoming a follower of Christ, and what is required after making our choice and commitment concerning Christ.

Development is the spiritual formation element of Christ's commission. Development involves providing the assistance and training Christ's followers require to progressively become more Christ like. Spiritual development must begin with the decision to abandon self-centeredness and adopt a lifestyle of sacrificial Kingdom of God service.

Jesus recruited followers with this challenge: "He (Jesus) said to all, 'If anyone would come after me, let him deny himself and take up his cross daily and follow me.'" Luke 9:23/ESV

The Apostle Paul, who was inspired by the Holy Spirit to write most of our New Testament and establish numerous churches, expressed his self-denial as "Dying to Self". "I have been crucified with Christ. It is no longer I who live, but Christ who lives in me. And the life I now live in the flesh I live by faith in the Son of God, who loved me and gave himself for me." Galatians 2:20/ESV

Spiritual formation training addresses the creation of Christlike character and conduct. The goal of every follower of Christ should be to glorify God by the manner in which we live, love, and labor (Matthew 5:16; 1 Corinthians 10:31). Spiritual formation includes tasks like:

- Learning to love others unconditionally and selflessly. 1 Corinthians 13 describes this type of godly love, as "Agape Love".
- Learning to live and labor by faith. Galatians 3:10-14

- Learning to trust and obey God; consistently choosing God's will over our own. Luke 22:42
- Adopting, developing, and manifesting the spiritual character traits referred to in the Bible as "Fruits of the Spirit". Galatians 5:22, 23
- Becoming doers of God's word rather than merely hearers. James 1:22-25
- Learning how to win at spiritual warfare. 1 Peter 5:8
- Learning about the purpose and priority of the Bible. 2 Timothy 3:16, 17
- Properly and consistently utilizing prayer. Ephesians 6:18
- Learning how to deal with our trials, tests, temptation, and sin. 1 Corinthians 10:13

This is only a partial, representative list of topics that need to be addressed by local church discipleship development training.

Deployment is the third element that needs to be provided for via comprehensive local church discipleship training.

Jesus trained His disciples in order to prepare them to take over His redemptive mission once He physically exited earth. On several occasions He sent His disciples out in pairs and groups to conduct ministry. They always reported back to Him for evaluation after completing their assignments. Matthew 10:1-7; 17:14-20; Mark 6:7-13; Luke 9, 10:1-20

Scripture makes it clear that although followers of Christ are not saved by our own works, we are saved for the purpose of continuing the redemptive mission Christ died on the cross to make possible (Matthew 25:14-30; Luke 19:11-27; Ephesians 2:8-10).

Every follower of Christ has been equipped and enlisted by the Holy Spirit to perform specific tasks in cooperation with the other members of their local church. 1 Corinthians 12 refers to local churches as "The Body of Christ". Every member of the church has a God-given function to perform, as is also true for every member of our physical bodies.

Church members require training to discover, develop, and properly deploy their gifts and calling as intended by the Holy Spirit.

One of the primary responsibilities of church leadership involves providing the training and assistance followers of Christ require.

"He (God the Holy Spirit) gave the apostles, the prophets, the evangelists, the shepherds and teachers, to equip the saints for the work of ministry, for building up the body of Christ." Ephesians 4:11, 12/ESV

During one period of my ministry, I served as a Pastor of Leadership & Ministry Development. Apart from Holy Spirit help, the success of local church ministry rises and falls based upon the quality and quantity of its leadership. You can't have effective local church ministries of any type without qualified servant leadership to guide, provide for, and protect them.

My role and responsibilities during those years of ministry was to enlist, equip, encourage, and do whatever else was required to maximize the success of those the Holy Spirit had selected to serve as local church leaders. What I partnered with God to accomplish during those years of service was incredibly successful, significant, and satisfying. By helping local church leaders do what the Holy Spirit had enlisted and equipped them to do, rather than attempting to find church members to do what the pastoral staff felt needed to be done, our church went about "Deployment Discipleship Training" as I believe Christ intended when He commissioned His church.

In order to maximize the success of servant leaders our church put into practice a multi-stage process. I firmly believe that each interrelated stage of this process was essential to starting, and sustaining, and maximizing the success of the leaders and ministries involved.

Stage 1   I provided discipleship training for two prospective servant leadership groups each year; once in the spring and once in the fall. These training groups were highly publicized within our church throughout the year. Each group was limited to six participants

I developed my own six-week servant leadership training process/curriculum drawing heavily upon the work of Christian leadership and discipleship authors such as John Maxwell, Aubrey Malphurs, Ken Blanchard, Phil Hodges, Dallas Willard, and Bill

Hull. Additionally, I met with each trainee at least once during their training to learn more about them and provide personalized assistance related to determining God's purpose and plans for their life and labor.

These training classes remained "high profile" within our church, and were creatively publicized. Graduation ceremonies were conducted for those who successfully completed the leadership training. Training servant leaders was caried out as our church's highest priority discipleship task.

Stage 2   Many of those who completed the training classes eventually provided leadership for existing ministries and new ministries based upon what they/we believed the Holy Spirit had enlisted and equipped them to do. During these years of ministry our church was able to redemptively, creatively impact our assigned area of mission responsibility in numerous ways I had never previously imagined.

Stage 3   I provided ongoing support for ministry leaders while they:

- Enlisted and trained their ministry teams
- Developed their strategic plans
- Obtained the facility and financial support they required to maximize the success of their ministries
- Properly promoted their ministry within our church and throughout our area of primary mission responsibility. One of the ministry teams we started assumed responsibility for marketing all our local church ministry.

Additionally, I made myself available to provide assistance, counsel, encouragement, and mentoring for ministry leaders as they carried out their leadership responsibilities.

Stage 4   I regularly met with ministry leaders to evaluate the effectiveness of their various ministries. What's expected must be inspected, and corrected as required.

It is essential for local churches and local church leaders to establish, continually monitor, and maintain priorities that are aligned with Christ's "Main Thing" for His church. For "Making Disciples" to actually remain any churches "Main Thing" it must be center stage; not merely one of the things we do but the primary reason for our existence.

Local churches should understandably be concerned about social, political, and emotional/physical health issues but all of these are secondary concerns. None of these are intended by Christ to become our "Main Thing". Christ came to search for the lost and restore them to a right relationship with their Creator. Repeatedly, amidst the many miracles He performed and His profound teaching of truth, Jesus reminded His followers, "The God-given mission I have come to earth to accomplish involves diligently searching for and saving lost sheep (sinners)" (Luke 15:1-7; 19:10; John 3:17; 6:28, 29; 12:47). That is the mission Christ entrusted to His church before departing earth. Jesus did His part by sacrificing Himself for our sin. Christ's church has been entrusted with the responsibility of continuing His sacred spiritual mission through the redemptive strategies we employ to deal with secular societies physical, political, emotional, and relational problems.

Saving sinners includes helping them become devoted disciple followers of Christ. Jesus wouldn't allow anyone to follow Him for long who refused to obey Him.

"If anyone loves me, he will keep my word, and my Father will love him, and we will come to him and make our home with him. Whoever does not love me, does not keep my words. And the word that you hear is not mine but the Father's who sent me." John 14:23, 24/ESV

"Why do you call me 'Lord, Lord,' and not do what I tell you?" Luke 6:46/ESV

"Not everyone who says to me, 'Lord, Lord,' will enter the kingdom of heaven, but the one who does the will of my Father who is in heaven. On that day many will say to me, 'Lord, Lord, did we not prophesy in your name, and cast out demons in your name, and do many mighty works in your name?' And then will I declare to them, 'I never knew you; depart from me, you workers of lawlessness.'" Matthew 7:21-23 ESV

I encourage everyone reading this article to obtain a copy of "The State of Discipleship". This 2023 report jointly produced by The Barna Group and The Navigators describes what is currently taking place in local churches throughout the United States related to discipleship. I would also encourage you to obtain a copy of the book I've written and published titled, "Christ's Discipleship Deal."

For assistance with local church discipleship and/or servant leadership ministry please contact me through my ministry website: www.newlifeguyde.com

DR. STEVEN GEORGE COY

A TROPHY BUCK TALE
(Excerpted from *The Christian Outdoorsman*)

The reality of hunting the mountain alone loomed very real before me in the ghostly half-light of pre-dawn."

FOREWORD

This story was first published by the Boone and Crockett Club in the Fall 1995 issue of their magazine, *Fair Chase*. Edited versions were later published in the *Eastman's Journal* and the *Remington Country* magazine.

Here is, for His glory, "A Trophy Buck Tale"...

The dawn was barely awakening on the eastern horizon as I eased up the trail on the dry south end of the mountain ridge. I had located and glassed the ridge the previous day from the Gros Ventre River highway below.

My brother and hunting partner, Tom Coy, a Jackson fishing outfitter and owner of Coy's

Wilderness Float Trips was scheduled on a float trip down the Snake River. The reality of hunting the mountain alone loomed very real before me in the ghostly half-light of pre-dawn.

My intent was to find an area to effectively solo hunt by

glassing for deer and elk while bugling and listening for a bull to reveal himself. As it turned out, my sense of hearing was not going to be the key to success. It was the sense of sight that would uncover a trophy.

There are different ways to hunt big game. Sometimes experiencing the great outdoors with a close friend—one who loves the hunt and the experience as much as you—is very rewarding and memorable. Sometimes having three or four hunters pays off. Drives can be successful, and three or four sets of eyes often see more game than one or two—and there's the comradery, the jokes, the kidding. The tactics and methodology of a big game hunt can be diverse.

But sometimes there's nothing quite like being on top of a mountain alone. And being on top of a mountain with a very clear goal is even more exciting. To match wits with a magnificent bull elk, or to outsmart an aged mule deer buck that has survived more hunting seasons than most and has already beaten many a Nimrod at his hand is the ultimate challenge. The name of the game is focus.

One opponent in this age-old game is focused on sheer survival. For him, he either wins or he dies. There are never disappointments, and there is rarely a second chance. He gets good at the game by winning at an early age, then keeps on winning until he retires at the hands of natural elements, disease, a predator, or old age. Age inevitably catches up to even the best of every species.

For the other opponent in this game of focus it's also a case of survival—survival of the natural elements which are foreign to his existence most days of the year. To survive and conquer—that's the challenge for this two-legged creature. It's something primeval, something deep within the blood, something that stirs the soul at the approach of the autumn season.

This stirring is first conceived by a subtle change in the smell of the August air, accompanied by an almost imperceptible decrease in the length of the days. Trees and plants perceive the decrease and begin to respond with outward changes in appearance.

Soon the process has birthed full-blown in the inward parts of this wannabe conquistador. It's something a certain wife calls "the rut". It's the time when a man reaches for a weapon and begins to make plans to escape the humdrum of everyday life, and focus his human senses on a conquest of an age-old and very primitive nature.

There is something invigorating and exciting about entering a new hunt area for the first time. With each new appearance of virgin territory, the realization that your trophy could suddenly materialize before your eyes has a tendency to keep the adrenaline flowing full force.

With each step, pause, and listen, things sound right, look good, and the epitome of wilderness hunting is taking place. It's the stuff that makes the experience rewarding regardless of whether a game tag is filled, and in spite of the laborious physical demands that sometimes make the body scream as it is pushed to the limits.

The smell of autumn with its damp, golden leaves and crystal crisp air reminds you that it really is hunting season, and you really are where you want to be. This could be the day you've worked for, waited for, and dreamed of for many years—the day you bag and claim for your own a trophy bull or muley buck that beats all others you've ever harvested—a trophy that will find its rightful place above the fireplace where you've envisioned it for many seasons.

The area had every kind of niche required for good mule deer and elk habitat. There were pockets of aspen trailing up out of draws, there were mountain meadows filled with abundant forbes and grasses as well as patches of sagebrush, and there was more than enough dark coniferous timber where bulls and bucks seem to easily disappear after the intrusive sounds of opening day.

But maybe, you speculate in dreamy anticipation, just maybe no one has been here this season before you. Maybe you're the first, and the game will be relatively un-spooked...

As I slowly approached a new panorama of scenery, my eyes would rapidly scan the immediate area where an animal would be quick to react to my presence. If the approach is right, if the wind is right, and your stealth has been successful, it can happen that way. You see the animal before it sees, smells, or hears you. More often than not, game is first sighted in the distance with the help of good optical equipment.

Using my Bushnell Custom Compacts, I quickly scanned the far reaches of my field of vision dissecting the edges of timber on the far slopes, then scanning the open drainages for animals still trying to grab their last bits of forage before bedding down. Mature animals seem to retire very early into shaded areas for rest and concealment.

It was 7:30 in the morning. I had been still-hunting for well over an hour. It was the kind of country where you expected to spot game at any moment, yet with daybreak quickly slipping away the desire to see as much grazing habitat as possible kept me moving. It's a trade-off. Moving at this early hour allows you to see and glass more terrain, but the chance of being detected is increased dramatically with your sporadic though stealthful movement.

I had just slowly, ever so slowly, topped a knoll dotted with scrub pine and ground juniper that sloped to the west. Below me was an open grassy hillside that dropped a hundred yards to an aspen grove, then curled around to the north and dropped another hundred yards into more aspen. To my left less than 130 yards away was dark timber that stretched from the ridge I was on down into and south of the aspen pocket. I would allow my head and eyes to rise only enough to glass everything in view before slowly taking another half step forward.

Suddenly to my left and below me three sets of antlers seemed to rise out of tall grass adjacent to the dark timber. My first reaction was, "Three bucks". I slowly lowered my body and retreated in reverse out of the line of sight.

The thought flashed through my mind, "Maybe just some kind of dried weeds or thistle sticking up out of the grass".

I dropped to my belly and slid twelve feet forward behind a double-trunked fir tree. Easing to my elbows I quickly focused my binoculars on the "weeds". Yes! Three mature bucks were bedded contentedly in shaded tall grass chewing their cuds.

The distance was about 125 yards. It took me no time to make a decision. Though it would be a long haul out, bringing home a good buck would be well worth the effort, and there was still plenty of day left to continue hunting for a bull elk.

During that split moment of thought the deer on the right began to rise. It was time to quickly assess the choices and make a shot. My cool collectedness quickly disappeared as the animal rose to its feet, only one bound away from heavy cover. When the buck looked my way, still seemingly unaware of its stalker, I realized it was more than just a buck. It was the buck I had prayed for.

My 308 Remington was at my shoulder. The 3-9 power Leopold quickly found its target. I had solid rest front and back, but the cross-hairs settled slightly high. Rather than risk the time or movement of sliding a few inches forward, I cocked the butt of the rifle slightly higher on my shoulder. The cross-hairs settled behind the shoulder of the buck and I squeezed the trigger. *Ka-boom!*

At the sound and recoil of the rifle, I feared I had squeezed too quickly in my haste to fire before the animals winded me and spooked. My fear was quickly alleviated when I saw the animal collapse and unsuccessfully try to regain its feet. His two companions rose and stood gazing at their fallen comrade. Not moving or fleeing, both were good bucks, one appearing to be taller with more points than the downed buck, but not nearly as wide.

I waited and watched several minutes, relishing the moment and watching the bucks that didn't seem to want to leave. Nor did I particularly want to run them off. They at last slowly sauntered off, disappearing into the darkness of the timber.

When I reached the deer I realized he was a very good and symmetrical 5X5 buck. I conservatively estimated him to score 175-180 B&C points, with heavy tines and probably 5-inch bases. I gave humble thanks to my God and Creator who had allowed me to harvest such a beautiful animal.

After several pictures and self-portraits with my Olympus XA2 35mm camera, I field-dressed the buck and estimated a live weight of at least 250 pounds. Amazingly, I was absolutely calm and unexcited during the whole process. If I had known what the buck's antlers were going to score, my emotions would not have been nearly so stable. As it was, my mind was still concentrated on the second half of my prayer request.

I hunted for the next two and one half hours without seeing or hearing an elk. I saw one cow track on a trail through some aspen. It seemed the second half of my prayer request was not going to come to pass. However, my utter lack of disappointment is not hard to understand considering the trophy I eventually brought home.

I returned to my buck and spent the next hour caping and deboning. I was able to stuff the boneless venison into my backpack, which included portions from the front half and the back-straps from the rear half. The two hind legs were tied together at the hocks for strapping over my shoulder. With my belly bag (aka fanny pack), my rifle, a backpack weighing who-knows-what, two huge deer hams, a heavy two and a half foot-wide rack with head and cape attached, plus other miscellaneous gear,

I had my hands full to say the least.

Though I could transport the entire load, I could not move very far, perhaps thirty yards at a time.

I found the most efficient transport method to be hauling one half of the load fifty yards down the trail, then returning for the second half to haul a hundred yards down the trail, then returning again. In this seesaw fashion, I more or less traveled non-stop down the mountain for the next four hours.

I arrived back at my vehicle at 4:30 in the afternoon with my trophy on my back and a smile in my heart. I felt amazingly intact, though understandably exhausted, after five grueling days of mountain hunting and four grueling hours of packing out a trophy buck. It is amazing what the human body can do, even at age forty-five.

By the grace of God my body never experienced soreness or cramps during the days following, with the single exception of where the ropes carried the weight of the hams across my shoulders.

The buck eventually dry-scored 195 3/8 gross with a final net score of 192 B&C. The width was

28 3/4 inches. It easily made the next edition of the Boone and Crockett Club's Records of North American Big Game. The trophy was also honored by the North American Hunting Club as the largest typical mule deer taken by a member with rifle in 1992.

I've often wondered what makes us trophy hunters tick. The answer is not particularly obvious to us or to others. I suppose it has to do with the challenge of setting a goal and the pursuit of that goal. Perhaps it's the satisfaction of actually attaining the goal.

But one thing I guess I do know: The memories of the experience of a Trophy Buck Tale last a long, long time...

ABOUT THE AUTHOR

Steven George Coy was born, raised, and educated in Illinois before moving to the Rocky Mountains. After short stints in Colorado and New Mexico, he spent most of the next 25 years roamin' the hills and mountains of Wyoming. He now resides with his wife of more than 46 years in southwestern Colorado.

His extensive yet unique educational background includes a Bachelor of Science degree from Southern Illinois University in Natural Resource Management; two Master's degrees from the University of Illinois at Springfield—one in Biological Sciences with a major in wildlife mgt, and one in Psychology/ Counseling; and a Doctor of Ministry degree from Trinity Theological Seminary where he graduated summa cum laude (with highest honors) in 1987.

He is a writer, counselor, educator, teacher, husband, and father of two sons. He was a U.S. Department of Interior wildlife biologist in Wyoming for seven years, and a pastor for almost nine years. He has deep roots in the wide and wild expanses of Wyoming, from which much of his outdoor writing was birthed. He is an avid Christian outdoorsman.

This extreme and unique diversity of educational and professional background, along with a lifelong passion of pursuing the great outdoors, gives Dr. Coy a depth of experience and insight that well qualify him to pen and edit the exciting real-life tales contained herein.

And seeded throughout his writings is a deep-seated faith that continually acknowledges and seeks to glorify God our Heavenly Father, and the Lord Jesus Christ, to Whom this book is dedicated.

For your own copy of *THE CHRISTIAN OUTDOORSMAN*,
or to request a quote on quantity discounts, email us at
sgcoy7@gmail.com
or write:
TCO, 703 Hartman Road,

Cortez, CO 81321
You may also visit our website at:
www.TheChristianOutdoorsman.com

BOOK REVIEWS

Rated 5 of 5 stars by **Goodreads.com**

"...certainly helps the reader recognize the greatness of God..."

Rated 10 of 10 stars by **CBM** Christian Book Reviews
www.christian-book-marketing.com

"...a must-read for every outdoorsman"

Steven G. Coy is also the author of
CLIMBING THE MOUNTAIN
OF HIS HOLINES—
One Man's Journey of Communing
with Father God

LARRY CLAYTON

THE FIRST GREAT SERMON IN THE NEW WORLD: ANTON DE MONTESINOS, 1511

The greatest sermon in the more than five centuries since the discovery and settlement of the American continents by European explorers and conquerors was not preached in 1741 by Jonathan Edwards during the Great Awakening. "Sinners in the Hands of an Angry God" is indeed a stemwinder, but it was preceded by almost two and a half centuries by a sermon preached in 1511 in the city of Santo Domingo, today the capital of the Dominican Republic.

In 1510 a small group of four Dominican friars arrived on the island of Española (later the Dominican Republic). They quickly came to view the conquest and settlement of the Americas triggered by the first voyage of Christopher Columbus in 1492 as a world that had been turned upside down for American indigenous peoples, where justice, truth, religion, and morality were bent and mangled by the greed, prejudice, and immorality of the Spanish settlers.

The *Niña*, *Pinta*, and *Santa María*, Christopher Columbus's Ships in 1492

The Dominicans, astonished by the brutality and horror perpetrated by the Spaniards on the native Tainos, decided to act. They not only believed the truths of Christian Scripture, but they determined to put it into action, as the Apostle James wrote in his book "Do not merely listen to the word, and so deceive yourselves. Do what it says," (James 1:22)

It fell to one of these Dominican friars, Antonio de Montesino, to be the first European to throw light on "this demographic disaster" and "who tried to waken the consciences of his compatriots."[1]

The leader of the little group of four was Father Pedro de Córdoba. A tall man with a handsome presence, he was a native of Córdoba, born into a noble and old Christian family. He studied at the famed University of Salamanca (the Spanish equivalent of Oxford or Cambridge in the English-speaking world). He was—if there ever could be—a model Dominican, combining erudition and evangelism in similar portions, a man of God, not retired from the world to the reclusive confines of a monastery but working in the world.

Father Córdoba called his small group of friars together to deal with the abusive and barbarous relations between Spaniards and Tainos on the island. They faced the question: What to do?

Not only were terrible sins being committed by these Spanish "Christians," but Indian souls were also perishing daily, or had perished, for want of the Gospel. After they prayed, fasted, and meditated around the clock, they agreed to preach a sermon to tell the Spanish settlers exactly where they stood in Christ's view of things. And, because of the Spaniards' inhumanity and greed they would tell them exactly what their reward would be. It would certainly not be in heaven with Jesus.

---

[1] Introducción, Silke Jansen and Irene M. Weiss, eds and contributors, *Fray Antonio de Montesino y su tiempo* (Madrid and Frankfurt am Main: Iberoamericana and Vervuet, 2017), pp. 7-8.

Barbarity and Cruelty of Spanish Conquistadors that Anton Montesino Preached Against

Everyone understood. All agreed. Córdoba had them all sign a document, affirming the Dominicans' total agreement on the message. They then selected the best preacher among them, Father Montesino.

The Christmas season of 1511 was upon them, and Montesano's sermon was scheduled for the fourth Sunday of Advent, or just before Christmas itself. The Scripture reading chose was from the Book of John, 1:22-23.

"Finally, they [the Pharisees] said, 'Who are you? Give us an answer to take back to those who sent us. What do you say about yourself?'"

"John replied in the words of Isaiah the prophet. 'I am the voice of one calling in the desert, 'Make straight the way for the Lord.'"

The stage was set. So that no one would miss it, everyone, including the governor and all leading citizens, were invited. Word of the sermon was delivered to their very homes.

"A sermon will be preached in the principal church of Santo Domingo my lords," so went the announcement, "and we wanted you to know that much will be said of interest to you, and we much desire your presence." How could anyone resist such a pleasant invitation? But there would be no hiding the bright lamp of life and truth for these Dominicans. The sermon that Father Montesinos preached lit a fire of controversy that has not ceased to this day.

Montesino stepped up to the pulpit, read the Scripture reading, and continued with some innocuous remarks about the season of Advent. Then he moved on:

"In the words of Isaiah, the prophet, 'I am the voice of one calling in the desert, Make straight the way for the Lord."

The congregation gathered before him nodded at the reading. Montesino then expanded on what lessons should be drawn from what he had just read. Both Isaiah and John the Baptist he recalled for his listeners called people to repent to make way for the coming of the Messiah. Without repentance there was no forgiveness. And without forgiveness, the hardhearted were doomed to eternal perdition.

"There is a sterility of conscience among you on this island," Montesino continued, "and a blindness in which you live. You are in mortal danger of condemnation, not realizing the grave sins you are committing with such insensitivity. You are immersed in them and dying in them."

The Spanish settlers of Española were in danger of eternal damnation if they continued to plague and enslave Indians. They had to be warned, explicitly, with courage and absolute conviction.

Then, with everyone's attention now coming alive to what this priest was saying, Montesino hit full stride.

"I want you to know that I have come to this pulpit, I who am the voice of Christ on the desert of this island. And you had better pay attention, not just listen, but heed with all your heart and mind. For this this will be something you never heard before, the hardest, the harshest, the most terrifying news you ever expected to hear."

Murmurs filled the rustic "cathedral," a small place among the pantheon of the great cathedrals of Spain and Europe, but the word preached was more powerful than the awe-inspiring cathedrals of back home.

Montesino waited for the agitation to die down a bit. He continued.

"This voice," he started back softly, but grew more pronounced, "says you are in mortal sin. You live and die for the cruelty and tyranny which you inflict on these innocent people.

"By what right?" and Montesano's voice strengthened, "by what right and by what law do you hold these Indians such cruel and horrible servitude?"

"By whose authority have you made such detestable war on these people who lived peacefully in their lands?"

"How can you hold them so oppressed and exhausted, without giving them food or curing their illnesses? They die daily from the work you demand of them."

"Let me be perfectly clear. You are killing them to get the gold you so crave!"

Momentarily, Montesinos's hearers were stunned into silence by this prophetic indictment aimed straight at them.

"And who among you is taking care to teach them about God the creator? Who is baptizing them, leading them to mass, celebrating holidays and Sundays?"

Monteniso's voice grew louder, more condemning, asking questions that truly transcend time and place: "Are these not men? Do they not have rational souls? Are you not obliged to love them as yourselves? Do not you understand this? Do you not see this? How can you be in such a profound and lethargic sleep? Be assured that in your state you can no more be saved than Moors or Turks who lack and do not want the faith of Jesus Christ."

"Rest assured that in your present state," he told the shocked congregation, without Christianizing your Indians and providing restitution for all the ills imposed on them, "you Christians have no hope of salvation and are little more than infidels like the Moors."

Lewis Hanke, one of the great historians of the twentieth century, observed that "Montesino evidently astounded and shocked the colonists; never before, apparently, had the indoctrination on non-Christians who were living in Christian kingdoms been considered the duty of all Spaniards. Thus developed the first significant and public clash in America between the zeal for the propagation of the gospel and the greed for gold and silver among the Spaniards, who for centuries had been accustomed to an economy based to some extent on war booty wrested from the Moors.[2]

Father Anton de Montesinos Preaching His Historic Sermon in Santo Domingo, December, (1511).

"He left them dumbfounded," an eyewitness, Bartolomé de Las Casas, wrote. "Some were furious, others were incorrigible, some were saddened, but, as far as I could tell, none were converted."[3]

Montesino stepped down from the pulpit, head held high, unafraid. No matter how disagreeable, he told his hearers what God

---

[2] Lewis Hanke, *All Mankind is One: a study of the Disputation Between Las Casas and Juan Ginés de Sepúlveda in 1550 on the Intellectual and Religious Capacity of the American Indian* (Dekalb, Illinois: Northern Illinois University Press, 1974), p. 4.
[3] Lawrence A. Clayton, *The Iconic Bartolomé de las Casas, a Maker of the New World*, manuscript to be published by Boydell & Brewer, Suffolk, UK, 2024, p. 60.

told him to say, advised and counseled to some extent by his fellow Dominican companions.

He was, in that instant, a reminder of the prophetic tradition in the Judeo-Christian life, a prophet like Isaiah or Jeremiah, who spoke the truth in the face of the sin and hostility of their listeners, the Israelites in the Old Testament.

In a stupendously quotidian aside, Bartolomé de Las Casas in his description of the event mentioned that Montesinos and a companion friar then left the church and walked back to their straw hut for a lunch of cabbage soup, "without even any olive oil, which happened sometimes."[4]

To state the obvious, this was an extraordinary mixture of the sacred and the profane, between a moment that will live as long as man and history survive with the need to eat some lunch. Las Casas's description of the sermon and lunch by Montesino endows the event or narrative with a truth and a veracity that makes them even more credible. In other words, why write about cabbage soup when dealing with the eternal? because they happened.

Regardless of Montesino spooning up his cabbage soup without olive oil, the congregation he just addressed was left murmuring, barely able to finish the mass. They too went home for lunch, but it was a quick one for all. The leading citizens soon gathered at the home of Governor Diego Columbus to deal with this outrageous priest who had accused them of being destined to hell.

These accusations were not taken lightly. Governor Columbus was persuaded to do something, so he and the delegation of disgruntled settlers made their way to the modest monastery—little more than a hut really—and knocked loudly on the door, demanding to see the Vicar, Pedro de Córdoba.

"We want that priest who preached the sermon!" they shouted.

Córdoba said he spoke for them all. The mob was not mollified and once again demanded to see Montesino. Córdoba stood his ground. Speak to me or not at all. He might have been a simple priest, but he was both a Dominican and of high birth back in Spain. They counted as much, if not more, as sauntering and strutting

---

[4] Bartolomé de las Casas, *Historia de las Indias*, V, p. 1762,

around out here in the wilderness of the New World, or the Indies as the Spanish called the Americas.

Columbus and the others began to back down. We just want to know they told Córdoba how Montesino could have preached such a prejudiced, insulting sermon, such a disservice to the king, accusing all these fine citizens of supposed sins.

How was it that Montesino told them they could not have the Tainos awarded to them by Queen Isabella, who had since passed away? The settlers had won the island and subjected its unbelieving people into submission so they could be instructed in obedience and the faith. They demanded a retraction.

Montesino and Córdoba listened quietly. If no retraction were forthcoming the governor added ominously, "we will remedy things ourselves."

The gauntlet was thrown down. Córdoba looked at them gently, not sternly like he felt. Deal with them as Christians he was thinking, even if they were an outrageous mob lying to us.

Córdoba calmly informed the delegation that Montesino represented the sentiments of all the Dominicans quite clearly and with the approval of all of them. He told them we have been sent by the King to these islands to preach the gospel and the truth. And the truth was that both Spaniards and Indians were perishing daily, the settlers for treating the Tainos as if they were mere animals and the Indians for lack of hearing the Word and accepting the Faith.

Córdoba may have been thinking of the Apostle Paul's letter to the Romans, "consequently, faith comes from hearing the message, and the message is heard through the word about Christ," (Romans 10:17)

The settlers were not mollified or persuaded by Córdoba's answers. They were even more obstinate in the face of this priest's insubordinate righteousness. They demanded Montesino retract his accusations, and, if not forthcoming, then all the Dominicans could start packing their bags to return to Spain.

The gauntlet was thrown down at the sandaled feet of these mendicant friars by the new lords of the land. At issue was none other than the power of God versus the power of the world. It is no different today.

Córdoba could not resist a bit of wit at this threat to send the Dominicans packing on the next fleet to Spain.

"Truthfully, sirs, packing won't take much effort." All their worldly possessions could be fitted into a couple of small trunks.

Faced with such an intrepid spirit, and indeed the power of the Church, the governor and others backed down and accepted Córdoba's promise to have Montesino return to the pulpit next Sunday. What a surprise was in store for the smug settlers wishing to put this priest in his place, even if he was a vicar of God.

Expecting a public retraction, they packed the small church to see this priest humble himself before the notables of the island. Montesino—no doubt in close collaboration with his fellow friars—chose as his Scripture Job 36, verses 3 and 4:

I get my knowledge from afar;

I will ascribe justice to my Maker.

Be assured that my words are not false;

One perfect in knowledge is with you.

Once the Scripture was read, Montesino ceremoniously closed the Bible and turned to face the congregation. In fact, most of the city's Spanish citizens were packed in.

"Let me turn to what we covered last Sunday," Montesino began. "Those words you found so bitter to take, they were in fact the truth."[5]

The listeners knew where the priest was going, and it was all they could do to suppress their anger. Montesino was not meekly retracting and conforming to their wishes. Not only did the Dominican ratify his message of the week previous but he also told his hearers that they would not be offered the Sacraments unless they repented and, furthermore, ceased their evil against the Tainos. And no doubt warmed by the sound of his voice and given courage by

---

[5] HI, V, p. 1766.

the content of his message, Montesino added that they could complain to Spain if they desired.

"We are serving God for sure, and it's no small service to the King as well." With that parting shot, Montesino stepped down from the pulpit and took his place in history at one of its most crucial junctures, the discovery, conquest, and settlement of the New World.

A multitude of questions arise at this juncture.

What power had these lowly appearing Dominicans over their haughty, conquistador hearers? Theologically, legally, philosophically, what did Montesino's sermon represent?

Meanwhile the Spanish conquest of the Indies spread to islands like Cuba and Puerto Rico, and then to the mainlands of Mexico and to Central and South America.

For us today it is sufficient to recall for the moment that along with the conquistadors came the priests and friars of the Catholic Church. It was a church corrupted by power and non-Scriptural beliefs and practices and in need of reform. So, it is not unusual that a contemporary of Montesino was a German priest, a member of the Augustinian order, Martin Luther. His call for reform and change in 1517 became the clarion call for reform and restoration of true values and teachings of Christianity according to Scripture and the Word of God in the Bible. He, in fact, kicked off the Protestant Reformation. But that for another time!

JERRY McRAVEN

JESUS IS THE ANSWER

John 14:6 (KJV) Jesus saith unto him, I am the way, the truth, and the life: no man cometh unto the Father, but by me.

Janice and I were in Farmington not long ago, when we saw a man with a sign asking for money. Janice was driving, and she stopped to give him some money. There was another man across the street who was also asking for money, and Janice went to him and gave him something as well. When Janice got back into the car, she informed me that she told them this: "Whatever your problem is, Jesus is the answer."

If you analyze what Jesus is saying in *John 14:6*, then we must know and understand that He is the "only" way, and He is the "only" truth, and He is where all life comes from.

Jesus is the Creator of all life, He is also the Creator of the Universe. He is our personal Savior. There are no other creators of life, only Jesus. Since it was Jesus who created everything there is in the Universe, then we must be aware of the fact that only Jesus has the answers to everything. After all, who knows more about the structure of a house than the one who built it? Who knows more about repairing an engine, than the one who built and designed the engine? It was Jesus that created everything there is, and He said Himself, that He was the "way." This means that He is the only way, there are no others. No one else has the answers that only Jesus can know.

If this is not true, then Jesus is lying to us, and His word says that He is incapable of lying. After all, what would God have to lie about? He's God! God can prove anything He says.

Jesus is also, "the life." This means all life came from Jesus. There is no other source of life. Jesus created the river of life, as well as the tree of life. And He breathed life into Adam and Adam came alive.

As the creator of all things, Jesus has the ability to do anything He wishes with His creation. He is also not limited to the creation; He lives outside of it.

Can you imagine, God opened the mouth of a donkey to speak to a man? How did God do this? The donkey didn't have to learn the language, he was not required to take voice lessons! But he spoke!

When Elijah was hiding from King Ahab, God sent him to the brook named Cherith. There God told Elijah he could drink from the brook.

This is what God told Elijah: "**1 Kings 17:4 (KJV) and it shall be,** *that* **thou shalt drink of the brook; and I have commanded the ravens to feed thee there."**

Again, how does one command a bird to procure food and take it to someone? Do you know anyone that is able to just command a raven or any other bird to do something like this? How does someone give directions to a bird? Maybe a GPS? Well, our Creator knows how to do such things! Jesus didn't need to give the ravens a map. The ravens didn't take the food to the wrong person, did they?

When Simon Peter needed to pay his taxes, Jesus gave him these instructions: **Matthew 17:27, "Go thou to the sea, and cast an hook, and take up the fish that first cometh up; and when thou hast opened his mouth, thou shalt find a piece of money: that take, and give unto them for me and thee."**

It is hard to come up with an answer as to how Jesus knew about this fish and the coin, other than to say He is God, and He is omniscient, which means He does actually know everything.

Our human brain comprehension has difficulty in dealing with such precision and mental capacity as this. We can't comprehend God's abilities. Perhaps Jesus just "spoke" to the fish to do what He did.

We find again, in the book of Jonah, where God speaks to an animal. In this case, it was the great fish that had swallowed up Jonah. Jesus knows how to communicate even with fish!

Jonah 2:10 (KJV), "And the lord <u>spake unto the fish</u>, and it vomited out Jonah upon the dry *land*." Such a monster fish as this released Jonah right where God directed him.

God even instructed Moses to speak to a rock one time. **Numbers 20:8, "Take the rod, and gather thou the assembly together, thou, and Aaron thy brother, and <u>speak ye unto the rock</u> before their eyes; and it shall give forth his water, and thou shalt bring forth to them water out of the rock: so thou shalt give the congregation and their beasts drink."**

Although Moses decided to "smite" the rock, instead of speaking to it as he was instructed by God, water did emerge from the rock as God said.

Even in the new testament Jesus said this about rocks: **Luke 19:40 (KJV), "…and he answered and said unto them, I tell you that, if these should hold their peace, the stones would immediately cry out."**

Again, such as this is difficult for us to imagine, but I would presume the Creator of all things, knows His creation and understands it better than we do.

We see things such as these to be "miracles." But with God, they are simply commonplace. God can call things that be not as though they are.

When people begin to think they are capable of doing what God does, and that they can call things that be not as though they were, they become gods.

After all, it was God quickening the dead and calling things that be not as though they were in Romans 4:17, not Abraham. Check it for yourself.

God never gave us the ability to create with our mouths. We can't speak anything into existence. We can't give life. We don't make animals talk either.

As a matter of fact, most animals won't even listen to us at all. Aren't you glad to know that during the millennium, this will all change!

In Genesis 22, Abraham was in need of a sacrifice, as he was not really desiring to sacrifice his son Isaac.

Genesis 22:13 (KJV), "And Abraham lifted up his eyes, and looked, and behold behind *him* a ram caught in a thicket by his horns: and Abraham went and took the ram, and offered him up for a burnt offering in the stead of his son."

In this case, Jesus provided exactly what Abraham was in need of. He needed a sacrifice, and that is precisely what Jesus provided for him.

Years earlier before Abraham even had a son, it was his desire to have a son to take over for him after he was gone.

Jesus appeared to Abraham and Sarah and prophesied to them their hearts desire. **Genesis 18:10 (KJV), "And he said, I will certainly return unto thee according to the time of life; and, lo, Sarah thy wife shall have a son."**

It isn't difficult for the originator of all life to speak a child into existence within a woman's womb. And it matters not if the woman is too old.

In the book of Numbers, there were some that decided to challenge the authority of Moses and Aaron as to only being God's leaders. God therefore, asked for all these elders to submit their "rods" to be kept overnight, and He would show through them, who He wanted to be in charge.

We must keep in mind, these rods were nothing more than tree limbs or sticks that were used for walking and for identification purposes. They have long been dead and no longer alive.

As a result, an old, long dead stick or rod, during the overnight hours, belonging to Aaron, not only bloomed flowers, it also produced almonds.

This action silenced those that thought to bring a challenge to the leadership of Moses and Aaron.

When Israel desired to have meat to eat, the next morning the camp was covered with quail. Where did they come from?

Where did the manna that they ate for 40 years come from? How did their clothes not even wear out for 40 years while they wandered in the wilderness?

How did Gideon defeat an army of 135,000 with only 300 men? What was the source of all the plagues that God used against Egypt? How does a river turn to blood? How does a country get overrun with frogs? Do you think God spoke to the frogs? I don't see why not, he spoke to fish, birds, and a donkey.

How did Jesus defy our laws of physics, and walk on the surface of water? How did Jesus heal lepers, or how did He raise the dead?

Could the fact that Jesus is the way, the truth, and the life have something to do with it?

Could the fact that Jesus is the Creator of the entire Universe be a factor in all of this?

Job said this about our creator God: **Job 26:7 (KJV), "He stretcheth out the north over the empty place,** *and* **hangeth the earth upon nothing."**

Well, as we all know, the earth isn't suspended upon anything, it just hangs on nothing in space. How does Jesus do this?

And how did Job know anything about this? How did Job know there was a huge "empty place," in the heavenlies? There were no telescopes back then.

I guess maybe God can also speak to us. What do you think? If we are open to God's Word, and we believe in Jesus as the way, the truth, and the life, maybe He can even speak to us.

We must remember what God said to Isaiah: **Isaiah 55:8 (KJV), "For my thoughts** *are* **not your thoughts, neither** *are* **your ways my ways, saith the lord."**

Part of this seems to be rooted in the fact that Jesus is the way, and apart from Him, we are all lost.

Apart from Jesus, we have no truth, and apart from Jesus, we have no life. He is the way, truth, and the life.

If this world is to survive, we must come back to the only way that has been afforded to us. That way being Jesus Christ. The only way. After all, there is no other way for us to survive apart from Jesus.

Saul was on the road to Damascus, and he thought he was in the right "way." He was convinced and determined that Christianity needed to be stopped. And he was trying his very best to accomplish this.

You could say that Saul saw the light. He met Jesus, and his name was changed to Paul. He found the true "way." This experience was Paul's answer. And Jesus changed his life forever. Paul as a result became the champion preacher of the resurrection. What Paul needed to hear, was the truth. Well, not only did Paul hear the truth, he met "the Truth" in person. Jesus Christ is the truth and He made Paul free!

Today, we are living in a world of lies, i.e., "There are many pathways to God," "All holy books are equal," "God has many names," "Satan does not exist," "There is no hell, and Jesus isn't the **only** way to God." To believe such heresies as these, our society has no chance but to be destined to failure and to hell. What we are seeing is the culmination of a society being totally indoctrinated by the educational system of the world. We now have a generation that has been shown "another way."

John 10:1 (KJB), "Verily, verily, I say unto you, he that entereth not by the door into the sheepfold, but climbeth up some other way, the same is a thief and a robber."

We know Jesus is the door to heaven and the Father because He said He was. And He is the only way to the Father. Anyone that tries to get there in any other way, is a thief and a robber. Jesus is that way.

This world is trying to get to the Father without the aid or guidance of Jesus Christ, who is the only way to the Father. And they are failing miserably!

Jesus said in **Matthew 7:13 (KJV), "Enter ye in at the strait gate: for wide *is* the gate, and broad *is* the way, that leadeth to destruction, and many there be which go in thereat:"**

This is what we are witnessing in our society today. It seems that people are choosing to go another way to get to the Father or to heaven. Jesus tells us that this broad way leads to destruction.

I remember what Janice said, "Whatever your problem is, Jesus is the answer." That is such a fundamental truth. Because it matters not what we are facing, or what our problem is, the answer is still Jesus.

The challenge we have, is this: "Do we have enough faith or trust in Jesus to show us the way?" Or, will we just bypass Jesus and look for another answer.

Some of the problems you may have facing you today may look large but, Jesus has the perfect solution for everything if we will just trust in Him. Sometimes the solution may not come in the way you want it to, but we must trust in Jesus. After all, Jesus is still the way. God's ways are not always the same as ours. We can't forget that.

I can't imagine Gideon asking God for "Just 300 men to attack the Midianites!" I can imagine him asking for a million men or more! I need a million man army!!!

Jesus is the way, Jesus is the truth, and Jesus is the life. If we are to reach the Father, it will be through Jesus that we do, not anyone or anything else.

There may be a multitude of ways to solve a problem.

And as Joshua said, "For me and my house, we will serve the LORD." Well, me and my house will seek God's way to find a solution to our problems. We will pray and seek God's guidance. We will also believe that Jesus will speak to us a solution. The answer we get may not be the one we expected, but, we have to trust in Jesus and believe in Him.

I don't know, but maybe God wants to reach someone at the hospital, and He has sent certain individuals from this church or another to show them the way.

Maybe God has placed someone to be at a senior center to help someone find their way to God. God can even use a truck driver to show someone a map to their eternal destination.

God can show fifteen-year-old teen age boys, or girls, how to reach the lost in school and in sporting events.

Jesus can send in money; Jesus can heal our bodies. He can touch hearts of stone; He can find us jobs; He can use us to witness. Jesus can save our families, and He has the answer to all of our problems!

None of the problems we have now will go to heaven with us! They will be forgotten and nevermore to be remembered. Jesus had the answers all along.

Jesus can use you to be a part of someone's answer to a prayer! Jesus used a little boy and his meager lunch to feed multiplied thousands.

For whatever problems we encounter in this life, they all have the same solution or answer. His name is Jesus, the way, the truth, and the life!

CHELSEA KONG

EXPERIENCE GOD'S PRESENCE

This has been one of my favourite topics. Moses saw God face to face and experienced His glory. We may not experience a burning bush, but the Lord will show Himself to us when we seek Him. Joshua was always in God's presence and never left the tent unless God sent out to do an assignment that the Lord had given him. He made himself available to God. Moses waited on God for His instructions when the Lord brought him to Mt. Sinai and gave him the 10 Commandments. The Lord had carved out and written on. During the 40 days and 40 nights in Exodus 24:28, Moses had no food or water. Moses stayed at the moment a second time for 40 days and 40 nights. His face shone with God's glory. The glory changes us inside and out. The more time you spend in God's presence, the more transformed you become. You also need faith to believe that God will bring you into His presence. God made a promise to Moses about His presence going with him and that he will have rest in Exodus 33:14.

The Lord gives us satisfaction and desire for more of Himself. It is about building a relationship with God, Jesus, and the Holy Spirit. I have a book on this topic and it explains how to do this with examples from the Bible. It is a teaching guide and there are exercises included. I learned to love the Lord more when I got to know Him personally. Abraham is called God's friend. He knows God and spoke to Him daily.

Satan likes to deceive people into thinking that God's presence and the power of the Holy Spirit are evil. Believers miss out on encountering God when they believe in the lies. Jesus warns us in Matthew 12:31 not to blaspheme the Holy Ghost or there will be no forgiveness.

There is a key to stay in God's presence requires that we keep ourselves free from unrepentant sin and unbelief in God. King David prayed to the Lord daily. He asked the Lord to cleanse him of all his sins. Jesus told us when we pray to forgive and he told Peter to forgive 70x7 according to Matthew 18:22. We can boldly come before the Lord (Hebrews 4:16).

This verse applies to those who are already in Christ. When we have repented and asked God to forgive us for all sins, then He will hear and answer us. He will forgive us of all our sins. Abide with Jesus through constant forgiveness and you will experience His presence daily. God's presence dwells where He is praised, worshipped, and adored. A healthy fear of God keeps a man humble from sinning. Be aware of God every moment of the day and constantly speak and listen to Him whenever you can.

I learned about hearing God's voice and practiced listening after being baptized in the Holy Spirit. I spend time reading the Bible, praying, singing songs to the Lord, and then wait for Him to speak. I write down what He said or sometimes record it. I felt God's presence when I sang and waited on Him. He reveals Himself differently to each person. I visualized my conversations with the Lord by faith when I first started. Then spontaneous thoughts would flow. I had a conviction within that I knew it was God. If we allow Him, He will speak many things to us. I have a book about How to Hear God's Voice.

I felt the Lord's presence and knew that He was with me. I felt His love, peace, and joy in my heart. He also would bring healing not only physically but also emotionally and mentally. We have to repent of our sins and to ask the Lord to cleanse us by the blood of Jesus.

I sometimes focused on the Tabernacle. Then I let God lead me. Give thanks to the Lord for what He has done. Declare scriptures of God's promises. After singing for a while, I would feel the Holy Spirit inside me and I received new songs etc., to speak out. Sometimes I would also dance. I felt the atmosphere shifted. I was so focused and engaged. It became conversational in song. I enjoyed it so much that I didn't want to leave. I felt as if I wasn't even in my room anymore. God's presence can manifest to become rich and thick. I have experienced the manifest presence of God, mainly in my home when I am alone. When the presence of God is thick, it has weight to it and often people found themselves not able to move their body. The weight is so much that the body feels so heavy. There are people that don't feel God's presence. It depends on their relationship with the Lord and how He wants to reveal Himself to them. The key is to desire to know Him, have a relationship with Him, and to desire to remain in His presence. Holy Spirit will help us.

It is easier to live by walking by the Holy Spirit. I also serve in my church as a worship leader and during the worship, I would experience God's presence manifested. I would sing and then the anointing would flow. The atmosphere will change and then new songs, prophetic words, and prayers would come. When I dance, I would also experience exhilaration and fast movements with the streamers and flags, even jumping up and down. I had exuberant joy and moments of tehillah תְּהִלָּה (praise, song of praise) at home and in church. I became excited and engaged. Sometimes I felt like I was fighting while I danced. Some churches call this warfare dancing. When I prayed for people, they would feel God's presence. The Lord would reveal things to me about the person and tell me what to say to them, but they had the conviction in their spirit that it was a message from the Lord. There was one sister that had a neck injury and I prayed for her neck. I could feel God's power through my hands into her neck. The sensation was like a fire. There was a time I became so hot during time of prayer. The gymnasium at the time was actually cold, and it was wintertime. I had to take the coat off. The Lord reveals Himself and there are other experiences that I have had.

In His presence, He reveals His plans through visions to me. I have several in these past years that really affect me. I was praying with a friend and the Lord showed me the throne room in heaven with its glassy floor. I recall seeing my friend praying with his head covered with a shawl. Jesus was there and had a prayer shawl to cover his head and he knelt down by him and he called to me to come also to pray, so I came and I covered my head with a prayer shawl. Another time, Jesus showed me the earth below the glassy floor and I could see space and there were lights glowing around the world. All the believers around the world when they are seeking the Lord. He visits them. Another there, I saw a field of wheat ready for harvest. The sun was shining its rays so brightly in golden light. The wind was blowing across the field and then I saw millions of people with their arms raised in the air towards heaven. It is the end time harvest of souls and God's glory. There is one funny vision where I saw a serpent that had his fangs removed, so he had no fangs. I knew God punished the devil. There are dreams of strategy and prophetic dreams. Sometimes I had dreams of revival with a few churches full of people and people that I know. You can also have multiple spiritual gifts. You can read from Joel 2:28 and Job 33:14-17 regarding God speaking through dreams, visions, and prophesying.

People will know that you have been with the Lord. When they see you, your face, the way to talk and carry yourself is different. Your character gets transformed, and so are your thoughts. Your heart and the way you live your life are different. The more transformed you become, the less they recognize who you are. They will realize that you are a new person and they don't know the new you. In 2 Corinthians 3:18, we are changed to become like Jesus in increasing glory.

I also received the gift of writing books, creative writings, songs, poems, ideas, and more after spending time with the Lord. Holy Spirit gives and increases the gifts. Bezalel and Oholiab were anointed with the gift in all kinds of artist designs to create what was required for the Tabernacle (Exodus 31:2-6). Hiram from Tyre made various things for the Temple, as mentioned in 1 Kings 7:13-45. God's presence filled the Temple so the priests couldn't enter it (2 Chronicles 7:1-2). Receive God's wisdom, knowledge, and understanding and learn to abide in His presence.

Chelsea Kong is an author, creative arts and digital media artist, skilled administrative professional, payroll professional, and podcaster. She lives in Toronto and graduated from Hotel and Restaurant Management, Digital Media Arts, and Office Administration. She also has served in her local church in a variety of roles. She also has a passion for families being united. Her writing consists of children's books, puzzle books, stories, teaching series, poems, lyrics for songs, words of encouragement. She is the author of How to Hear God's Voice, Knowing God, Jesus, and Holy Spirit, etc. Her podcast channel is called ChelseaK. Chelsea has been aired on UnityLive Radio, The Lady Tracey Show, and on How to Live your life for Christ with George Calleja. She has an article on ReadersMagnet for Author Lounge and is highly recommended by

A Proud Christian blog and featured in YourAuthorHub. Her books can be found on Amazon, Barnes and Noble, and Smashwords.

https://chelseak532002550.wordpress.com

Knowing God
How to Hear God's Voice
New Life in Jesus
Loving Israel
God's Gifts/Spiritual Talents
Meeting God
Word Power
Fruit of the Spirit
The Tabernacle
Bride for Jesus
A Life of Prayer
Live Free
Who am I in Jesus
Walk in Love
God's Favor
Man of God
Woman of God
How to Use Money
God's Wisdom
Fasting
See Jerusalem and Bethany
First Fruit Offering
Feast of Trumpets
Day of Atonement

Coming soon:
The Blessing
Revival
Chelsea Learns Hebrew
Chelsea's Psalms and Poems
Give Thanks

Thanksgiving
Jesus Birth
Smokey the Cat
Passover Unleavened Bread
Resurrection Life

Teaching Series
How to Hear God's Voice Teaching Guide & Audio Book
Relationship with God, Jesus, Holy Spirit Guide
Knowing God, Jesus, Holy Spirit Guide & Audio Book
Flowing in the Prophetic

Teaching (Non-Sale on the website)
Purim
Passover
Resurrection

Made in the USA
Middletown, DE
20 August 2023